THE CAPILLARIES OF CHRIST

THE CAPILLARIES OF CHRIST

Understanding the Part You Play in His Body

Marty Mitchell

Nihil Obstat: Vy. Rev. James S. Lentini, V.F.
                     Censor Librorum

Imprimatur: Most Rev. William E. Koenig, D.D.
                     Bishop of Wilmington
                     March 10, 2023

The Capillaries of Christ © 2023 by Marty Mitchell. All rights reserved.

Printed in the United States of America

Published by Author Academy Elite
PO Box 43, Powell, OH 43065
www.AuthorAcademyElite.com

All rights reserved. This book contains material protected under international and federal copyright laws and treaties. Any unauthorized reprint or use of this material is prohibited. No part of this book may be reproduced or transmitted in any form or by any means, electronic or mechanical, including photocopying, recording, or by any information storage and retrieval system, without express written permission from the author. The only exception is brief quotations in printed reviews.

Library of Congress Control Number: 2022915967

Paperback: 979-8-88583-129-1
Hardback: 979-8-88583-130-7
E-book: 979-8-88583-131-4

Available in hardcover, softcover, e-book, and audiobook.

Scripture texts in this work, unless otherwise indicated, are taken from the New American Bible, revised edition (NABRE), © 2010, 1991, 1986, 1970 Confraternity of Christian Doctrine, Washington, D.C., and are used by permission of the copyright owner. All Rights Reserved. No part of the New American Bible may be reproduced in any form without permission in writing from the copyright owner.

Scripture quotations taken from The Catholic Edition of the Revised Standard Version of the Bible (RSV-CE), copyright © 1965, 1966 National Council of the Churches of Christ in the United States of America. Used by permission. All rights reserved worldwide.

Excerpts from the English translation of the Catechism of the Catholic Church for use in the United States of America Copyright © 1994, United States Catholic Conference, Inc. -- Libreria Editrice Vaticana. Used with Permission. English translation of the Catechism of the Catholic Church: Modifications from the Editio Typica copyright © 1997, United States Conference of Catholic Bishops—Libreria Editrice Vaticana.

Excerpts from the Second Vatican Council documents are from Vatican Council II: Constitutions, Decrees, Declarations—The Basic Sixteen Documents, edited by Austin Flannery, OP, © 1996. Used with permission of Liturgical Press, Collegeville, Minnesota. Excerpted from *The Mystical Body of Christ: A Timeless Portrait of the Church from a Beloved Catholic Evangelist* by Fulton J. Sheen. Copyright ©2015 by Ave Maria Press®, Inc., P.O. Box 428, Notre Dame, IN 46556, www.avemariapress.com. Used with permission of the publisher.

Any Internet addresses (websites, blogs, etc.) and telephone numbers printed in this book are offered as a resource. They are not intended in any way to be or imply an endorsement by Author Academy Elite, nor does Author Academy Elite vouch for the content of these sites and numbers for the life of this book.

DEDICATION

To my dear Mother. Mom, I will always cherish the faith relationship we share, the times we spend together expressing and growing in our faith, and the guidance I receive from the Holy Spirit through you. It is these special times and your unceasing prayers that have been an enduring source of encouragement, wisdom, and confidence for me while writing this book.

CONTENTS

A Note to You—the Reader xi
Acknowledgments xv
Introduction—A Bird's Eye View xix

PART 1
CREATION

Chapter 1: Conception 3
Chapter 2: Circulation 11
Chapter 3: Connection 19

PART 2
CONTEMPLATION

Chapter 4: Unique 31
Chapter 5: Destiny 49
Chapter 6: Potential 61
Chapter 7: Unified 69

Part 3
CULTIVATION

Chapter 8: Nutrients 83
Chapter 9: Nourishment 103
Chapter 10: A Healthy Heart 123
Chapter 11: Good Fruit 139
Chapter 12: Little Greatness 157

Part 4
COLLABORATION

Chapter 13: As Yourself 171
Chapter 14: In Communion 187
Chapter 15: Never Alone 199

Part 5
COMMISSION

Chapter 16: Be Alive! 215
Chapter 17: Be Holy! 225

APPENDICES

Notes 237
About the Author 257

A NOTE TO YOU— THE READER

When the Holy Spirit first put on my heart to learn more about the Body of Christ and my role, I did what you would probably do. I googled every variation of these words to see what I could discover. I quickly found millions of hits discussing the Body of Christ with varying degrees of detail, clarity, and theological and scriptural backing.

When I narrowed the search to include the role individual Christians play in this Body, I had difficulty finding anything with much specificity written from Catholic sources or perspective. There were many entries written from Protestant and non-denominal Christian perspectives. However, these were primarily high-level one-page blog or website posts that weren't all that comprehensive.

I thought there must be books on the subject, so off to Amazon I went, only to find that I was sadly mistaken. To my surprise, I found nothing that would help a wondering Christian like me discover the part we play in the Body of Christ and God's unique purpose for us in this life.

Jesus, in the Holy Spirit, led me on a seven-year journey through the Body of Christ that allowed me to piece together what my role is in His Body. He took intricate care to show me my uniqueness and that of all God's children. Because we are wonderfully made, this uniqueness is central to the plan He has for each of us, and He wants us to use the unique gifts and talents He gave us to play our part in our creative way.

There are certain areas within His Body all of us need to focus on, though. These spiritual and physical activities became clear to me as I learned what is necessary for the health and growth of His Body. As my journey proceeded, I could sense God was laying everything out for me so I would share it with you and others.

What took me seven years to piece together and another three years of doing research for this work, I am grateful to present to you in this book designed to help you discover, reinforce, or build upon the part you play in the Body of Christ in whatever stage of faith and life you reside.

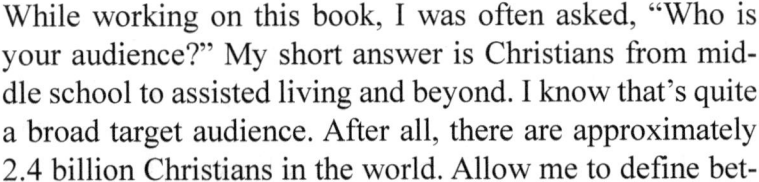

While working on this book, I was often asked, "Who is your audience?" My short answer is Christians from middle school to assisted living and beyond. I know that's quite a broad target audience. After all, there are approximately 2.4 billion Christians in the world. Allow me to define better what I mean. This book is for you if you are a:

- *Devoted Christian* in any stage of life because your gifts and talents and your role in the Body of Christ are constantly evolving.
- *Wondering Christian* (like me) trying to find your purpose in life and wanting to figure out if you are on the right path (I'll always be wondering).
- *Desiring Christian* looking for more out of life.

A NOTE TO YOU—THE READER

- *Down or dispirited Christian* who doesn't realize how uniquely blessed and loved you are and who may need a boost to your self-worth.
- *Uncertain Christian* looking for clarity and direction on your spiritual journey.
- *Distracted Christian* who wants to practice your faith with better attention and intention.
- *Fallen-away Christian* who needs some help rejuvenating your faith.

Can't we all relate to some of these characterizations? Our faith can ebb and flow as we move through the different seasons of life. I'd say every one of these describes me at different times in my life. As you read this book, I hope you will become better aware of and grow in your understanding of God's plan and purpose for you, wherever you are in life. I also pray this book will help you cultivate a plan of your own for playing your unique part in the Body of Christ with intention every day.

FINAL NOTE:

In this book, you will see references to the human body and the Body of Christ. For clarity, as the text goes from one to the other, body with a lowercase "b" will refer to the human body and Body with an uppercase "B" will refer to the Body of Christ.

DISCLAIMER:

I am not a priest, pastor, minister, deacon, or member of the clergy in any respect in any church. I am not a theologian or a biblical scholar, nor have I had formal education in the same. I do not write or speak for the Catholic Church. I am not a medical doctor, nor do I have an educational background in the medical field. I am a member of the laity who has been on a spiritual journey to draw closer to God, and I share what I have learned on this journey so it might help you along in yours.

—Marty Mitchell

ACKNOWLEDGMENTS

To You Most Holy Trinity, Father and Son and Holy Spirit, the one true God who is the inspiration for every word seen on these pages. I offer You my deepest gratitude for choosing, trusting, and allowing me to be the vessel You are using to send this message into the world. This has only been possible because of Your guiding presence and generous provisions.

To my family, you have always been a great source of love, support, and encouragement, especially as I battled through emotional challenges, a cancer diagnosis, and spinal surgery while writing this manuscript. Thank you to my Mom, my son Darren, my brother Scott, my sisters Kathy, Sue, and Michele, and your families. I derived great strength from your prayers for and belief in me. Thank you also to my Dad for his prayers in heaven. Special thanks go to Kathy, who quickly edited the ancillary materials with great care.

To my Mom, Gina, my sister Sue, and my lifelong friend Frank Graviano—my patient and dedicated beta readers as I completed each chapter. I am forever grateful for your thoughtful feedback, corrections, and suggestions and for sticking with me throughout. Special thanks and gratitude go to Frank who waited until Part 4 to tell me about his dislike for reading!

To my parish pastor, Very Rev. John B. Gabage, V.F., I must also thank you for your support, insight, prayers, and the ministration of the sacraments, all of which blessed and sustained me while writing this book.

To the entire Author Academy Elite and Igniting Souls team—I joined you in July 2019 with only a concept in mind and no idea how to turn those thoughts into a book proposal, much less a published work. I want to express my profound appreciation to my publisher and coach, Kary Oberbrunner, and to all the writing coaches with whom I had the pleasure to work and learn from on both the live and the recorded calls. Specifically, I must mention Kary, Daphne V. Smith, Abigail Young, Nanette O'Neal, and Tony Colson. Special thanks to Andrea Porritt Fehr who helped turn my rough outline into harmonious book parts and chapter titles that gave me clarity and direction through the writing process. And to Niccie Kliegl, my faith-based business coach. Working with you while and after writing the manuscript was the best thing I could have done. I am grateful for all you are and do.

To the supportive, encouraging, and passionate group of authors and creators we know as the Igniting Souls Tribe. It is such a pleasure to work alongside each of you and it has been an inspiration to see your dreams and stories come to life. Special thanks to my accountability partners along the way: authors Crystal Waltman, Vona Johnson, and Dana Lyons, all of whom pulled me through when things

ACKNOWLEDGMENTS

felt overwhelming or gently lit a fire under me when I was slacking.

To my editor and high school friend, Chris Caldwell. Thank you for your valuable and faithful perspective and direct feedback, edits, and suggestions. I owe you a debt of gratitude for your gracious help with this work.

Book Cover Design: AshtonD

Author Photos: Maureen Porto Studios

INTRODUCTION— A BIRD'S EYE VIEW

For twenty years, I set off from my home on Maryland's Eastern Shore at 3:30 a.m. for a fifty-mile commute to my downtown office. I soon found that the serenity of the pre-dawn, the silence, and the light traffic volume were a great prayer opportunity. I often lost myself in prayer only to realize that I had driven several miles down the interstate without any recollection. In prayer or otherwise, I am sure you can relate!

I began contemplating and praying about the Body of Christ at one point during this period. Baptized as an infant, I went to parochial elementary school, received my First Holy Communion, and proceeded through CCD (Sunday school) into middle school in preparation for the Sacrament of Confirmation. I remember learning that Jesus is the head and the Church is the Body.

Decades later, I felt the desire to understand this concept more thoroughly. There were a lot of questions that kept coming to mind. What is this Body of Christ? It is a challenging concept to grasp. What does the church teach about it? How does it function? How is the Holy Spirit involved? If the Church is the Body of Christ, what is expected of it?

This concept was an even more difficult thing to understand on a personal level. Hey, I am a member of my local parish. I've been baptized. If the Church is the Body, does that mean I am a member? Do I have a role to perform in this Body? If I do, it would be nice to know what that is. I wanted to know if I was living in a way that helped this Body function in a healthy manner. What is expected of me? What part do I play?

> Faith…is a gift that lasts our whole life, but bears fruit only if we play our part. [1]
> —Pope Francis

God's answers often come in unexpected ways and are always on his timeline. One morning as I drove to work, the sky was filled with clouds, and dawn was breaking. As the sun rose from the horizon, the radiant rays filtered out from behind the clouds like a folding hand fan snapped open at full attention.

Waves of thoughts started to come to mind, blessing me with something of an epiphany. I was inspired to zoom out to take a high-level view of the Earth. Looking down, I envisioned all the highways and streets of the world filled with vehicles, all speeding in various directions. I could see the sidewalks connecting the expansive city blocks with people scurrying around from one place to another.

From this bird's eye view, it dawned on me that this scene looked surprisingly like the human circulatory system. The highways represented veins and arteries. The secondary roads, side streets, and sidewalks signified the tiny capillaries. The vehicles and people symbolized blood cells, each with a different function, rushing through these circulatory vessels carrying oxygen and other nutrients through the bloodstream to the extremities of the body, or the far-reaching corners of the world.

This visual allowed me to better understand the Body of Christ. We, all baptized Christians, are members of this Body, each with a specific purpose conceived by God, led by Jesus (the head) and carried out in union with the Holy Spirit (the heart and soul) through His gifts and fruit and our unique God-given gifts and talents.

> A body is an organic whole, composed of an intimate number of cells and members, all directed by the head and all vivified by the soul and all directed to a common end, which is the conservation of the organism and its ultimate happiness.[2]
> —Fulton J. Sheen, *The Mystical Body of Christ*

Visualizing the Body of Christ in this way was helpful; however, I still needed to satisfy the questions I had about my specific role. I continued to search for clarity through scripture. I consulted what few spiritual works and writings there are on the subject. The Catholic Catechism was a valuable resource on the concept and structure of the Body of Christ, although not as much on a personal level. I soon realized it was hard to find books that offered insight into what individual Christians can do to perform our unique role in this Body.

I continued to read the Bible and contemplate the words of Jesus, the apostle Paul, and others. I listened for the Holy Spirit as He gave me direction and guided me as I asked for and sought answers. I was led closer to the saints and learned how some lived. I studied the writings of modern-day spiritual scholars and leaders.

The more I read and listened, several recurring themes kept coming to mind that helped me to understand the Body of Christ and the role individual Christians play in it more clearly. I will share this instruction and themes as we journey through the Body of Christ.

What I just explained was the genesis of this book. Who better to speak on this subject than Jesus, His apostles, the Saints, and modern-day theologians? Thought-provoking Scripture verses and quotes help the reader contemplate God's plan for them and understand their part in this Body.

Part 1: Creation-This takes you through the biblical conception of the Body of Christ, presents some fantastic facts about the human circulatory system, and ties the two together; this is a recurring theme throughout the book.

Part 2: Contemplation-Transitions to helping you realize that you are unique, that God has plans for you to reach your earthly (and eternal) destiny, and that you are well equipped to fulfill your role.

Part 3: Cultivation-Practical ideas and examples of how to put what was discovered in Part 2 into practice, helping you to envision and plan the part you play in the Body of Christ.

Part 4: Collaboration-You are not in this alone. Great things happen when Christians work together to be the hands and feet of Christ. When we do it in unity with the Holy Spirit, we can move mountains.

Part 5: Commission-This will inspire and motivate you to intentionally play your part in the Body of Christ every day so you will receive and reflect His light, love, and joy.

The Capillaries of Christ is a message of love and Christian unity. The message of the Gospel is love, mercy, and salvation. The commandments all point to love. God is Love. We are all made in His image and likeness. If we do good and love, we will be fruitful members of the Body of Christ and living in the kingdom of God.

PART 1

Creation

> For as Christ, who is the Head of the Church, was conceived by the Holy Ghost in the womb of the Virgin Mary, so now the Church, which is His new Body, is conceived by the same Spirit in the womb of humanity.
>
> —Fulton J. Sheen, *The Mystical Body of Christ*

Important Note: In this book, the terms "the Body of Christ" and "The Mystical Body of Christ" refer to the Church. These terms have been used interchangeably over the centuries. This is an essential distinction in the Catholic Church because there are times when "the Body of Christ" is strictly used to refer to Jesus' physical body, his offering on the cross, and most specifically, the Blessed Sacrament of the Eucharist—in which we receive "the Body of Christ." All references to "the Body of Christ" herein pertain to the Church.

1
CONCEPTION

When the time for Pentecost was fulfilled, they were all in one place together. And suddenly there came from the sky a noise like a strong driving wind, and it filled the entire house in which they were. Then there appeared to them tongues as of fire, which parted and came to rest on each one of them. And they were all filled with the Holy Spirit and began to speak in different tongues, as the Spirit enabled them to proclaim.

Then Peter stood up with the Eleven, raised his voice, and proclaimed to them, "You who are Jews, indeed all of you staying in Jerusalem. Let this be known to you, and listen to my words." Those who accepted his message were baptized, and about three thousand persons were added that day.

—Acts of the Apostles 2:1-4, 14, 41

And so it was that the Holy Spirit descended on the disciples, and the new Church was formed. In the words of Benedict XVI, "At Pentecost, the Spirit of the risen Christ created the beginning of the new humanity, the new community, the Church, the Body of Christ."

The apostles were ordinary men of diverse backgrounds who, along with the Blessed Mother and other disciples, received the Holy Spirit and were sent into the world to proclaim the Good News of the cross, the resurrection, and the ascension.

These followers saw the signs and miracles that were evidence of Jesus' divinity. They heard the word of God spoken directly from the lips of Jesus. They listened intently to their teacher as He told parable after parable to help them begin to understand the kingdom of God.

These men reclined at table with Jesus at the Last Supper. Jesus washed their feet. Except for Judas Iscariot, they were the first people to receive Holy Communion (taken together, the texts of Matthew 26 and John 13 suggest Judas departed beforehand). Eleven now, they watched from afar while Jesus was falsely accused, tried, convicted, persecuted, and tortured as He endured His Passion. They agonized over his crucifixion and were some of the first disciples to whom Jesus revealed Himself after He rose from the dead.

"Jesus came and stood in their midst" in the locked Upper Room (John 20:19). They touched His wounds. They saw the resurrected Christ eat a meal. The risen Lord cooked them breakfast on the shores of the Sea of Galilee. They saw Him appear to the masses. Jesus instructed these men on what to do when He left this Earth. They saw Him ascend on the clouds as he was taken up into heaven.

These were the hand-picked eyewitnesses of Jesus' three-year ministry while in this world. They were the eyewitnesses of His humanity and His divinity.

Apostolos, the Greek origin of the word apostle, is translated "sent forth." Another meaning is messenger. Jesus, upon appearing to His disciples in the Upper Room, told them:

Peace be with you. As the Father has sent me, so I send you.

—John 20:21

These witnesses, these messengers, these apostles, filled with the power of the Holy Spirit, were sent forth by Jesus into the world to build the Church He established through the Word of God spoken from His lips, by His sacrifice in dying on the cross, and by rising from the tomb.

THE CHURCH

What exactly is the Church? The traditional meaning of the word church is twofold. When associated with Christianity, it can refer to the building where public worship takes place or to a body of Christians worshipping in a building or constituting one congregation. An individual can be a member of a church.

"The word Church refers to the people whom God calls and gathers together from every part of the earth. They form the assembly of those who through faith and baptism have become children of God, members of Christ, and temples of the Holy Spirit" (*Compendium: Catechism of the Catholic Church* 2006, para. 147; [CCCC]).[1]

In Christianity, there is the Catholic Church, the Orthodox, and the various denominations of Protestants. The Catholic and Orthodox are rightly identified as the Church (separated by schism over authority, not doctrine) while the denominations of Protestants, and their congregations, are identified as Ecclesial Communities.

According to Catholic doctrine, these Ecclesial Communities, "because of the absence of the sacramental priesthood, have not preserved the genuine and integral substance of the Eucharistic Mystery [and] cannot . . . be called 'Churches' in the proper sense."[2]

Since the time of Jesus, divisions and doctrinal differences have separated the non-Catholic Christian denominations from the Catholic Church. However, "men [and women] who believe in Christ and have been truly baptized are in communion with the Catholic Church even though this communion is imperfect."[3]

Despite this imperfect communion, all Christians, by faith and proper baptism into Jesus Christ, are part of the Body of Christ and brothers and sisters in Christ (*Catechism of the Catholic Church* 2nd ed., 1994; [CCC]).[4]

Over the centuries, there have also been many offshoots formed as independent Christian congregations. It would be well beyond my knowledge and understanding to know the beliefs and practices of these independent congregations in the U.S. and worldwide. As such, it is also beyond the scope of this book. When referring to Christians in the pages of this book, I include the Catholic Church, the Orthodox, and the mainline Protestant denominations.[5] There are many others that I also include based on the validity of their baptism, as I discuss below.

The foundational belief of Christianity is in the trinitarian God—the Father, the Son, and the Holy Spirit—that Jesus Christ is the Messiah, the Savior of the world, conceived by the Holy Spirit, born of the Virgin Mary, suffered and died for the forgiveness of the sins of humanity, was buried, rose from the dead, ascended into heaven, and will come again in glory to judge the living and the dead (Nicene Creed). In this, most of the world's Christians are united.

Jesus Christ is the head of the Church. St. Paul explains, "He is the image of the invisible God, the firstborn of all creation. For in him were created all things in heaven and on earth, the visible and the invisible...He is before all things, and in him all things hold together. He is the head of the body, the church" (Col 1:15-18). As the head of the Church, Jesus is the head of the Body.

Christians, whether Catholic, Orthodox, or Protestant, are also united in another essential element—the sacrament of baptism.

"Baptism constitutes the foundation of communion among all Christians" (CCC 1271). As Christians, we are the Body of Christ. One becomes a member through baptism and faith in Jesus Christ. Whether Catholic, Orthodox, or Protestant all who have been baptized with water in the name of the Father, the Son, and the Holy Spirit (CCC 1238–1240), together with the proper intention of the minister "to baptize" and the one being baptized "to be baptized" (valid baptism),[6] have received the gift of the Holy Spirit. He is the same Spirit who descended on the apostles at Pentecost and who has been poured out to believers through the sacramental waters of baptism down through the generations.

Isn't it beautiful and comforting to know that we are all united in the one Holy Spirit who takes up residence in our hearts (Gal. 4:6)? We are each a temple of the same Holy Spirit.

Pope St. Paul VI indicated the Church "is the visible plan of God's love for humanity," because God desires "that the whole human race may become one People of God, form one Body of Christ, and be built up into one temple of the Holy Spirit."[7]

Fulton Sheen wrote, "Christ declared that they should become members of His body by being born of the Spirit," that is, through "the spiritual birth of the waters of the Holy Ghost" in baptism.[8]

The Body of Christ

Now that we know the Church is the Body of Christ, united by the Holy Spirit, let us delve deeper into the purpose of this Body. As Bishop Sheen wrote, "It is a body animated by a living soul – the Spirit of God."[9] This is important, for without the outpouring of the Holy Spirit, we are all individuals; with the Spirit, we are united as one. St. Paul expressed it this way:

> As a body is one though it has many parts, and all the parts of the body, though many, are one body, so also Christ. For in one Spirit we were all baptized into one body, whether Jews or Greeks, slaves, or free persons, and we were all given to drink of one Spirit. Now the body is not a single part, but many.
> —1 Corinthians 12:12-14

Jesus Christ is the head of the Church, the Holy Spirit is the heart and soul of the Church, and we, baptized Christians, are the Body of Christ with Jesus at the head and the Holy Spirit at the heart and soul.

The mission of this Body is to "make disciples of all nations" (Matt. 28:19), "to proclaim and establish the Kingdom of God begun by Jesus Christ among all peoples" (CCCC 2006, 150), to glorify God, and to bring the light of Christ into the world. As members of the Body of Christ, we are to spread the Good News (the Gospel) about who Jesus is and what He did for humanity when He laid down His life, shed His blood for our salvation, and rose from the dead.

As Christians, we are not only followers of Christ—He lives in and through us. St. Augustine is credited with having said:

CONCEPTION

> A Christian is: a mind through which Christ thinks, a heart through which Christ loves, a voice through which Christ speaks, and a hand through which Christ helps.

We are to witness His love in everything we say and do. We are to share God's abundant graces and love with others. We are to be a channel of His love, an instrument of His peace, and a reflection of His light. We are to obey God's commandments. We are to love Him above all things (Matt. 10:37–38), to love our neighbor as we love ourselves (Mark 12:31), and to do unto others as we would have done unto us (Matt. 7:12).

The Body of Christ is not only the congregation within the walls of the physical church building but also the outreach of the members in the local communities and to the ends of the earth. Each member's part in the Body is partly a function of the unique God-given gifts and talents bestowed on us by the Holy Spirit. It may be as a member of a particular church or community, an organization, or through personal contact with others.

God places us in contact with others and brings them into our lives, not out of happenstance but out of divine will. There are no coincidences with God. As we interact with others, we have an opportunity to play our part AND we are blessed to encounter Jesus in them and to be the recipient of the other person's role in the Body of Christ. How wonderful!

When we listen to the Holy Spirit and respond to Him, these occasions allow us to see the goodness in others and to show others the goodness in us, who is Jesus. St. Augustine also said, "This is the whole Christ, head and body, one formed from many . . . whether the head or members speak, it is Christ who speaks" (CCC 796).

Importantly, the Body of Christ is not only local, limited by only one generation, or constrained by a particular era. It expands throughout the world and "is the extension of the Incarnate Life of Christ through space and time" (Sheen 2015, 76). As individual members of the Body pass away, others are born through baptism and the outpouring of the same Holy Spirit; the Body of Christ is perpetually alive. It lives on forever until the end of time.

The Church is worldwide, a collection of believers "from every nation, race, people, and tongue" (Rev. 7:9). The Christian faith brings all baptized people together into one family. "So then you are no longer strangers and sojourners, but you are fellow citizens with the holy ones and members of the household of God" (Eph. 2:19).

We are on a unique path in this life and a unique spiritual journey. God has a unique plan and purpose for each of us, a unique part to play in his Body.

> For as in one body we have many parts, and all the parts
> do not have the same function, so we, though many, are
> one body in Christ, and individually parts of one another.
> —Romans 12:4-5

Now let us explore how the human circulatory system works, gather some amazing facts about blood cells and the vessels that carry them, and envision how this symbolism can help us understand our unique role in the Body of Christ.

2
CIRCULATION

This is the blood of the covenant which the LORD has made
with you according to all these words.
—Exodus 24:5–8

This cup is the new covenant in my blood,
which will be shed for you.
—Luke 22:20

The average adult human body has roughly
25 trillion red blood cells.

Throughout the Bible, blood is a continuous theme. In the Old Testament, "blood played an important role in the everyday life of the ancient Israelites. It was said that the life force of all living things was in their blood."[1] Animal sacrifice was customary. The blood was poured out on the altar and often sprinkled on the people in attendance, sealing their covenant with God.

These traditions continued during the time of Jesus. The Holy Family would make the annual trip from Nazareth up to Jerusalem for Passover. I wonder what Jesus thought when he saw thousands of lambs sacrificed knowing that He would become the sacrificial lamb for all of humanity when God's new covenant would be sealed with His blood, shed on the cross.

It is fitting, then, that we look to the human circulatory system and the flow of this life-sustaining blood to understand better what we, the members of the Body of Christ, must do to sustain the precious life of this Body while we are alive and passing through it.

God's creation is truly awe-inspiring. Sadly, we are so involved in living that we take so much of it for granted. We spend little time soaking it all in, realizing it, observing it, and expressing gratitude for it.

One of the grandest miracles of all is no further than our fingertips: the human body. There are many intricacies within each of us that keep us alive, allow us to reproduce, protect us from germs, heal our wounds, form our intellect, give us our senses, cleanse us, and give us strength, sturdiness, and mobility.

God created a world that sustains our bodies through the air we breathe, the water we drink, and the nutrients we ingest. He covered every intricate detail and left nothing out. We are profoundly phenomenal human beings; thanks be to God!

The Circulatory System

Life-sustaining blood is transported through the human body by the circulatory (or cardiovascular) system. The center of this system is the heart. It pumps the blood through a vast network of blood vessels that filter out through the entire body in what is referred to as a closed-loop system.

The blood is transported from the heart by the arteries and returns to the heart through veins. This transportation system resembles a tree.[2] The "trunk" is the main artery called the aorta. It branches into large arteries and then to progressively smaller and smaller blood vessels. Sound familiar? In the parable of the Vine and the Branches, Jesus says:

> I am the vine, you are the branches. Whoever remains in me and I in him will bear much fruit, because without me, you can do nothing.
>
> —John:15:5

At the end of this arterial progression are the most numerous networks of the tiniest vessels called *capillaries*.

"The capillary networks are the ultimate destination of the [oxygenated] arterial blood" from the lungs and "heart and are the starting point for the blood flow back to the heart" through the network of veins.[3] The University of Minnesota Atlas of Human Cardiac Anatomy states: "An extraordinary degree of branching of blood vessels exists within the human body which ensures that nearly every cell in the human body lies within a short distance from at least one of the smallest branches of this system: a capillary."[4]

The vast expanse of the capillaries supplies oxygen, other nutrients, water, glucose, and gases in the blood to the body tissues. They also pick up carbon dioxide and waste products to carry them away from the tissues into the veins for the trip through the kidneys and liver (to eliminate waste) to the heart and lungs for the release of carbon dioxide (exhalation) and to be loaded up with oxygen before being sent out by the heart through the body again.

THE CAPILLARIES

According to several medical article sources, in an average adult body, it is estimated that there are ~25 billion to 40 billion capillaries, each with an individual length of one millimeter.[5] If every one of them were lined up end-to-end, it would stretch over 100,000 miles.[6] That is more than four trips around the earth!

There are several types of capillaries. For this book, I will be referring to the true capillaries.

The smallest blood vessels in the body, the capillaries are about 8 to 10 microns (0.001 mm) in diameter, just large enough for red blood cells to pass through them single file.[7] The vessel wall is just one cell thick.

The diffusion of substances through their thin walls allows the capillaries to perform their function. According to healthline.com, "Their single layer…makes capillaries a bit 'leakier' than other types of blood vessels. This allows oxygen and other molecules to reach your body's cells with greater ease."[8] This permeability allows for an exchange in the body tissue where oxygen, gases, water, and nutrients exit the vessels and carbon dioxide, water, and waste enter.

"The network of capillaries is known as a capillary bed. The fluid that leaks out of the capillaries is known as interstitial fluid. It is this leaked interstitial fluid that bathes your body cells in nutrients."[9]

Have you ever wondered why your skin turns white when you put pressure on it? Because it presses the blood out of the capillaries, leaving a whiter appearance when the pressure is released. How about birthmarks? They appear due to the dilation of the capillaries.[10] Why do we immediately bleed when cut? The capillaries.

BLOOD CELLS

Fifty-five percent of human blood consists of a watery straw-colored fluid called plasma. "The main role of plasma is to take nutrients, hormones, and proteins to the parts of the body that need them. Cells also put their waste products into plasma. Plasma then helps remove this waste from the body. Blood plasma also carries all parts of the blood through your circulatory system."[11]

Three types of cells, each with a specific function, float in the plasma through the blood vessels. Red blood cells transport oxygen and carbon dioxide, white blood cells fight infection, and platelets stop bleeding after an injury by clumping together or clotting.

On average, men have approximately twelve pints of blood in the body, and women have about nine pints. The blood makes up roughly eight percent of the total body weight of the average adult and, according to various sources, takes about 20 seconds to circulate through the entire vascular system.

The red blood cells are the body's cellular lungs; their job is to take oxygen to every cell and deliver carbon dioxide to the lungs. Each second, we lose about 3 million red blood cells, only to be replaced by the same number produced in the bone marrow.[12] The body makes about 250 billion red blood cells each day.

"Adults have around 25 trillion red blood cells in circulation at any given time." If these lay on each other, they would reach more than 30,000 miles. "Red blood cells circulate on average for about four months"[13] before they degrade and die.

"White blood cells are the defenders of the body. Also called leukocytes, these blood components protect against infectious agents (bacteria and viruses), cancerous cells, and foreign matter."[14] The University of Rochester Medical Center's Health Encyclopedia indicates, "When your body is in distress and a particular area is under attack, white blood cells rush in to help destroy the harmful substance and prevent illness."[15]

Appropriately, the immune system and white blood cells are often considered the same. Physicians order blood diagnostics to check the level of white blood cells because it will inform them whether the body is battling "an underlying problem, such as infection, stress, inflammation, trauma, allergy, or certain diseases."[16]

There are five main types of white blood cells, each with a different responsibility in the immune system. As important as they are in sustaining life, "they make up less than 1 percent of total blood volume. The lifespan of a white blood cell varies from 18 hours to many years."[17]

The platelet component of blood stops bleeding. These blood cells circulate throughout the system, waiting to spring into action when an injury or other trauma damages a blood vessel. Once in the bloodstream, the platelets live for 8-10 days.

"A blood vessel will send out a [chemical] signal when it becomes damaged. When platelets receive that signal, they'll respond by traveling to the area and transforming into their 'active' formation. To make contact with the broken blood vessel, platelets grow long tentacles and then resemble a spider or an octopus."[18]

These cells clump, bind, or stick together to spread out over the damaged area in adhesion. If bleeding continues, more platelets are "called" to accumulate around the wound in the aggregation process. Collectively, the platelets collaborate to form the clot.

> How good to sing praise to our God; how pleasant to give fitting praise. The LORD rebuilds Jerusalem and gathers the dispersed of Israel, healing the brokenhearted, and binding up their wounds.
> —Psalm 147:1-3

The four main components of the blood each have multiple functions. Going even further, the five types of white blood cells are quite diverse, each performing an important responsibility, some even spawning other critical cells in the bloodstream.

Then there are four different blood groups, each determined by the presence or absence of different types of antibodies (proteins that scout out and lock onto foreign substances) and antigens (protein or sugar molecules on the surface of the red blood cells). Each blood group (A, B, O, AB) gets classified as positive (+) or negative (-) depending on whether a protein called the RhD antigen is present. The four groups have eight blood types, either + or -. Some are compatible; others fight terribly if transfused.

This multiplicity and diversity of blood cell function and type are orchestrated to perfection, united to sustain the life of the healthy human body. Capillaries are the vessels that facilitate the flow of this life-giving blood throughout the body. They form the highway down which the individual blood cells travel as they perform their unique function and play their part in the body.

Every person is on a unique life journey, just like the cells in the blood. "The blood flow through the capillaries plays such an important part in maintaining the body."[19]

Now let us tie together the Body of Christ and the blood flow in the human body in a way that will help to demystify and illuminate what it means to live, as St Paul often said, "in Christ"; that is, in his Body.

3
CONNECTION

> The Church is made up of a multiplicity of members,
> as the Body of Christ is formed of a multiplicity of cells.
> —Fulton J. Sheen, *The Mystical Body of Christ*
>
> The heart is an organ about the size of your fist
> that pumps blood through your body.
> —National Institutes of Health

Debbie was an avid runner in training for her fifth marathon on that bright September Tuesday morning. With the big race on the coming weekend, she worked in a longer training run before heading to her job in Manhattan's financial district a couple of hours later than usual. (This story is based on the experience of a former colleague; details adapted for this book.)

Debbie ascended from the subway beneath the Twin Towers of the World Trade Center at 8:39 a.m. After standing in line for coffee, she stepped on an elevator sometime after 8:45 a.m. for the ride to the 78th-floor express lobby of the North Tower. She never made it.

At 8:46 a.m., the first hijacked plane barreled through the massive structure like a guided missile about 95 floors up, severing many elevator cables. Debbie heard the explosion and felt her bones rumble, instantly sensing that her life was in peril.

Suddenly, her elevator car was no longer going up; it was in free fall. The release of adrenaline into her bloodstream triggered processes in her body that she would instantly need to rely on if she had any chance of escape. Unknowingly, her mental acuity sharpened, her strength increased, and her sense of pain diminished. Her heart pounded, pumping elevated oxygen levels into her lungs and through her body to aid in her flight from danger.

Debbie could see the horror on the faces of the other ten passengers with her. She could feel the heat from the inferno above. She could hear screams as the elevator fell past each floor landing. The tall, thin, twenty-something athlete could taste ash billowing down the shaft. She choked on the smell of jet fuel, melting steel, and burning flesh. She was on sensory overload, and she was no longer in control.

Abruptly and without warning, the elevator came to a jolting stop about three feet above the ground floor when the emergency brakes, the last remaining safety feature, engaged. The passengers were in varying degrees of physical distress. Debbie could come to her senses and had a heightened level of alertness.

After shaking off the jarring experience, she and several others attempted to pull apart the doors, now hot to the touch. The added strength and increased tolerance for pain were a Godsend for Debbie. She and the others were able to work together to open a space of about six inches, no more. Debbie was able to pry herself through and jumped to solid ground. Still in her running shoes, she ran, stopping once she reached Midtown, unaware she had run out of her shoes.

In what seemed like a split second, and obeying her sensory impulses, Debbie's life was saved before the Twin Towers crumbled.

JESUS—THE HEAD

The head is the central operation center where signals and directions are transmitted throughout the body to instruct how, when, and why we act. If the head separated from the body, the activity of life would cease. The eyes, ears, tongue, and nose send signals to the brain. The brain determines the appropriate response to the sensory input. The head leads the body into action.

As humans, our senses of sight, hearing, taste, and smell, our voice, bodily functions, and movements are all processed within and directed from the head, specifically in the brain. Inside the skull, the head houses all the sensory organs. It is where the sudden danger triggered the rush of adrenaline through Debbie's circulatory system, which allowed for the fight and flight that helped her survive. It is where Debbie's will to live was in accord with God's will for her escape from death.

Jesus, the head of the Church, is the head of the Body of Christ. Unlike any other physical or moral body (i.e., a nation, society, or club), this Body is Mystical, "something visible and invisible, something tangible and intangible, something human and something Divine" (Sheen 2015, 7). Jesus leads this Mystical Body, directing the creation, life, movement, and redemption of this living being throughout time. "Jesus Christ is the one whom the Father anointed with the Holy Spirit and established as priest, prophet, and king" (CCC 783).

And St. Paul expressed it this way:

> For in him were created all things in heaven and on earth, the visible and the invisible, whether thrones or dominions or principalities or powers; all things were created through him and for him. He is before all things, and in him all things hold together. He is the head of the body, the Church. He is the beginning, the firstborn from the dead, that in all things he himself might be preeminent.
> —Colossians 1:16-18

HOLY SPIRIT—THE HEART AND SOUL

Through the anointing of baptism, the Holy Spirit flows from Jesus, the head, into the Body, the Church (CCC 782). In one of his sermons, St. Augustine said, "What the soul is to the human body, the Holy Spirit is to the Body of Christ, which is the Church."[1] St. Thomas Aquinas wrote, "the head has a manifest preeminence over the exterior members; but the heart has a certain hidden influence. And hence the Holy Spirit is likened to the heart, since he invisibly quickens and unifies the Church; but Christ is likened to the Head in his visible nature."[2]

The Holy Spirit is the heart (2 Cor. 1:21–22) and soul of the Body of Christ. At Pentecost, the apostles (and other disciples - the Church at that time) were "sent forth" by Jesus in the Holy Spirit to spread the Good News and the light of Christ into the world. In the human body, blood is sent forth from the heart through the arteries and capillaries to nourish and cleanse every tissue and extremity of the body. In this analogy, the blood represents the Church.

The blood returns to the heart every twenty seconds to be replenished before being sent on another mission through the body just as the Church remains one with the Holy Spirit to be replenished with guidance, strength, clarity, and wisdom as the Body of Christ works the Spirit's wonders throughout the world.

Blood plasma carries every component of the blood to every tissue cell in the body. The Church carries Jesus to every corner of the world.

> Before all else, the Gospel invites us to respond to the God of love who saves us, to see God in others and to go forth from ourselves to seek the good of others.[3]
> —Pope Francis, *Evangelii Gaudium*

CHRISTIANS—THE BLOOD CELLS

The individual blood cells in the body represent every baptized Christian in the Body of Christ. Just as the blood cells perform different, life-sustaining functions, each of us is unique. No two are the same, each with a diverse collection of skills, abilities, and talents and on a unique path in life.

The blood cells respond to the pumping action of the heart. We are to respond to the nudging and prompting of the Holy Spirit. When various parts of the body need more oxygen and other nutrients, have wounds in need of binding, or have waste in need of being carried away, the blood cells are called by chemical signals to respond as appropriate.

As members of the Body of Christ, we are given signals by the Holy Spirit to be aware, listen, obey, and act. We are called to be saints, have sacrificial love, pray, love our neighbor, offer help, share each other's joys and burdens, and be involved.

Red blood cells carry oxygen and nutrients throughout the body. So do we by exercising the gifts and spreading the fruit of the Holy Spirit (I will discuss these more in Chapter 8) throughout the Body of Christ, ideally to everyone we encounter. Think of the gifts (wisdom, understanding, counsel, fortitude, knowledge, piety, and awe) as proteins (energy) that fuel our responsiveness to the Holy Spirit and the fruit (love, joy, peace, patience, kindness, generosity, gentleness, faithfulness, and self-control) as nutrients in the Body of Christ.

Red blood cells keep the body alive by bringing oxygen to every tissue and organ cell. Jesus breathed the oxygen of the Holy Spirit into his disciples when He first appeared to them after His resurrection.

> And when he had said this, he breathed on them and said to them, "Receive the Holy Spirit."
> —John 20:22

We keep Christ alive in the world through the Holy Spirit living in each of us as we bring Him to every life on Earth. "We are like letters sent by God. Our every encouraging word and caring deed can communicate God's love to the people around us."[4]

White blood cells defend the body from attack, infection, and illness. So do we by rising against the evil that surrounds us, crying out for Jesus when beset by temptation, repenting and confessing our sins, counseling others who may have fallen into sin, and praying for justice and Jesus' protection for ourselves and others.

> So submit yourselves to God. Resist the devil, and he will flee from you.
>
> —James 4:7

Platelets race to wounds, binding together to form a clot that stops bleeding. So do we by banding together to overcome trials and tribulations, by rushing in to help at the scene of an accident, by lending a hand during and after natural disasters, and by donating in charity according to our means just as the poor widow did when she "offered her whole livelihood," as Jesus said after she put her last two coins in the temple treasury (Luke 21:1-4).

We stick together with friends with whom we share similar interests. We bring together different capabilities. We know each other's strengths and weaknesses. Together, we can act in unison. St. Cyril of Alexandra wrote in his *Commentary on John's Gospel*: "For if Christ, together with the Father's and his own Spirit, comes to dwell in each of us, though we are many, still the spirit is one and undivided. He binds together the spirits of each and every one of us, . . . and makes all appear as one in him."[5]

The capillaries spread throughout the human body carrying life-sustaining blood to every tissue cell. They branch out to every extremity. These vessels form the circulatory highway down which the individual blood cells travel as they perform their unique functions.

The highway and roadway system on every continent connects the smallest towns and the most desolate populations to the major cities and the economic heartbeat of a metropolitan area. With 2.3 billion Christians globally in 2019,[6] the Body of Christ is connected to every corner of the world. These pathways perpetually allow Christians to be just steps from others to share the light, love, joy, peace, and face of God incarnate with them throughout the world. In other words, most people are within steps of a Christian called to holiness.

> No cell is so isolated that it is shut to the Lord. His love reaches everywhere. I pray that each one may open his heart to this love.[7]
>
> —Pope Francis

Capillaries can be recruited in response to a stimulus such as exercise to provide more oxygen to muscle tissues. When there are back-ups and delays on our roads and highways, we follow the detours offered by a phone app that brings other open pathways into our route to shorten the time to our destination. In the Body of Christ, "every grace received must furnish a highway along which the gospel of Christ shall have a straight and unimpeded path for propagation" (Sheen 2015, 218).

When there is a blockage in a blood vessel or other acute cardiac event, new vessels can form to bypass the disruption in the flow of life-giving blood. When there is a terrorist attack, natural disaster, or other significant trauma somewhere in the world, members of the Body of Christ answer the call for help. These events often open the door to new pathways of ministry, service, and love.

The diffusion of materials through the capillaries' thin walls enables them to perform their function. This permeability allows oxygen, nutrients, sugars, and water to exit and waste, carbon dioxide, and other gases to enter on queue.

Christians are not limited by boundaries either. "I can do all things in Christ who strengthens me" (Phil. 4:13). We are blessed with the opportunity always to be flexible enough to respond to God's will, not only for our lives but in the moment by dropping everything and following the Holy Spirit on the path of love.

The circulatory system performs intricately and flawlessly in the healthy human body to keep every cell in the head and body alive. The blood is sent forth by the heart to every extremity through the capillaries and returns to the heart like clockwork for replenishment.

The Church and her members, in unity with the Holy Spirit, are called to keep Jesus Christ, the Head of the Body of Christ, alive in the world. Christians are sent forth by the Holy Spirit to carry the light and life of the risen Christ into our communities and to the corners of the world.

> After this the Lord appointed seventy[-two] others whom he sent ahead of him in pairs to every town and place he intended to visit. He said to them, 'The harvest is abundant but the laborers are few; so ask the master of the harvest to send out laborers for his harvest. Go on your way; behold, I am sending you.
>
> —Luke 10:1–3

Healthy blood cells are always available to play their part. Are we?

In Part 2, we will realize how well-prepared each Christian is to do just that.

> What the soul is in the body, Christians are in the world.
> —Anonymous: from The Epistle to Diognetus

PART 2

Contemplation

The initial step for us all to come to knowledge of God
is contemplation of nature.
—St. Irenaeus of Lyons

The blood flow through the capillaries plays such an important
part in maintaining the body.
—Lynne Eldridge, MD., Verywellhealth.com

4
UNIQUE

> The human being is single, unique, and unrepeatable,
> someone thought of and chosen from eternity,
> someone called and identified by name.
> —Pope St. John Paul II

> Every blood cell has a unique function
> to perform in the human body.

At some point in your life, you undoubtedly met or knew someone with a personality unlike any you had ever encountered. Maybe that person had such a sense of humor that she always left you shaking your head and laughing as she walked away. Perhaps it was someone who was so insensitive and arrogant that he was hard to be around for more than short periods. It may be a cherished friend or family member who always makes you feel you are the most special person in the world.

Whatever the case, you have likely known someone extraordinary, one of a kind, a piece of work, or unlike anyone you have ever met. I have known a few people who were so unique that "God must have broken the mold" when He made them.

God the Father, our Creator and Ruler of all creation, breaks the mold with every human He conceives. As God told the prophet Jeremiah, "Before I formed you in the womb I knew you," (Jer. 1:5). The psalmist David wrote, "You formed my inmost being; you knit me in my mother's womb. I praise you, because I am wonderfully made; wonderful are your works!" (Ps. 139:13-14).

With 7.8 billion alive in the world today,[1] it is remarkable to consider no two people are exactly alike. Sure, in multiple births, there are identical offspring in appearance, yet no two siblings have identical personality traits, feelings, talents, or dreams.

Think about fingerprints. It is widely believed that no two people have the same fingerprints. According to the New York Times, identical twins "come from the same fertilized egg and share the same genetic blueprint. To a standard DNA test, they are indistinguishable. But any forensics expert will tell you that there is at least one surefire way to tell them apart: identical twins do not have matching fingerprints."[2]

Pope Francis said: "Each of your children is a unique creature that will never be duplicated in the history of humanity."[3]

Through the Holy Spirit, God has endowed each of us with a unique collection of gifts and talents. These gifts and talents are to be used to bring the light and face of Christ into the world and build up the Body of Christ. When we live a life of example focused on the Gospel and share our

God-given gifts and talents with this intention, we will attract others to live a life in Christ. St. Paul, in his First Letter to the Corinthians (1 Cor. 12: 4-7), said this regarding spiritual gifts:

> There are different kinds of spiritual gifts but the same Spirit; there are different forms of service but the same Lord; there are different workings but the same God who produces all of them in everyone. To each individual the manifestation of the Spirit is given for some benefit.

Although every Christian has unique qualities, personalities, gifts, and talents, the same Spirit bestows these in each of us. It is the same Spirit who endowed the apostles with the gifts, talents, courage, and trust that allowed each of them to fan out to "make disciples of all nations, baptizing them in the name of the Father and of the Son and of the holy Spirit," as Jesus charged them to do with this Church mission before He ascended into heaven (Matt. 28:19).

The apostle went on to describe some of the spiritual gifts and graces in 1 Cor. 12: 8-11:

> To one is given through the Spirit the expression of wisdom; to another the expression of knowledge according to the same Spirit; to another faith by the same Spirit; to another gifts of healing by the one Spirit; to another mighty deeds; to another prophecy; to another discernment of spirits; to another varieties of tongues; to another interpretation of tongues. But one and the same Spirit produces all of these, distributing them individually to each person as he wishes.

The gifts St. Paul spoke of here most likely related to those bestowed on himself and the early successors of the apostles in the budding church in Corinth "because they are ministries and gifts which help to build up the community."[4] Clergy down through the ages were likely blessed with some of these spiritual gifts. It may be more difficult for you and me to relate to having the power of healing, mighty deeds (miracles), prophesying, and speaking and interpreting in tongues.

It isn't an all-inclusive list of gifts, however, not by far. And not all are called for these specific purposes in the Church, for St. Paul also taught this:

> Now you are Christ's body, and individually parts of it. Some people God has designated in the church to be, first, apostles; second, prophets; third, teachers; then, mighty deeds; then, gifts of healing, assistance, administration, and varieties of tongues.
>
> Are all apostles? Are all prophets? Are all teachers? Do all work mighty deeds?
> Do all have gifts of healing? Do all speak in tongues? Do all interpret?
> Strive eagerly for the greatest spiritual gifts.
> —1 Corinthians 12:27-31

The gifts and talents given to each of us are wide-ranging and diverse, uniquely bestowed, and equally as important in the Body of Christ as those about whom St. Paul wrote. Many modern-day Christians are blessed with some of the gifts listed above, and by the grace and initiative of God, they will use these gifts to build up the Church.

In Romans 12:6-8, St. Paul wrote: "Since we have gifts that differ according to the grace given to us, let us exercise them: if prophecy, in proportion to the faith; if ministry, in ministering; if one is a teacher, in teaching; if one exhorts, in exhortation; if one contributes, in generosity; if one is over others, with diligence; if one does acts of mercy, with cheerfulness."

Discovering Your Gifts and Talents

By God's grace, we have all been blessed with a unique gift or set of gifts and talents. St. Paul instructs us to "exercise them" by ministering to (serving) others, teaching, encouraging in faith, leading with diligence, and being merciful, cheerful, and kind. From the notes on Romans 12:6 (NABRE), "Everyone has some gift that can be used for the benefit of the community. . . . It is not an instrument of self-aggrandizement. Possession of a gift is not an index to quality of faith. Rather, the gift is a challenge to faithful use."

St. Paul encourages us to identify and use our gifts in a way that brings others closer to God and helps them see the face of Jesus more clearly. The gifts entrusted to us must be used to glorify God, spread the Gospel message of love and salvation, and bring the light of Christ into the world. This is our responsibility. Do you realize and recognize your gifts and talents?

When Moses went up Mount Sinai with two stone tablets as God told him, even God expressed a few of His characteristics:

> The Lord came down in a cloud and stood with him there and proclaimed the name, "Lord." So the Lord passed before him and proclaimed: The Lord, the Lord, a God gracious and merciful, slow to anger and abounding in love and fidelity.
>
> —Exodus 34:5–6

As Christians, we are brothers and sisters in Christ. While we are united in Jesus Christ through the one Holy Spirit, we are all unique. We are all made in God's image and likeness, yet each of us possesses unique personalities, qualities, character traits, strengths, weaknesses, abilities, talents, desires, passions, skills, experiences, and dreams.

In contemplating our gifts and talents, let's consider sisters Martha and Mary from the New Testament who, along with their brother Lazarus, were close friends of Jesus. Jesus often stayed with the family in the town of Bethany at the foot of the Mount of Olives just east of Jerusalem. The story of Martha and Mary is a familiar one; to set the scene, we go to Luke 10:38-42:

> As they continued their journey he [Jesus] entered a village where a woman whose name was Martha welcomed him. She had a sister named Mary [who] sat beside the Lord at his feet listening to him speak. Martha, burdened with much serving, came to him and said, "Lord, do you not care that my sister has left me by myself to do the serving? Tell her to help me." The Lord said to her in reply, "Martha, Martha, you are anxious and worried about many things. There is need of only one thing. Mary has chosen the better part and it will not be taken from her."

In what most biblical scholars say is St. John's account of the same gathering, John 12:1-3 gives us a bit more insight into the sisters' personalities:

> Six days before Passover Jesus came to Bethany, where Lazarus was, whom Jesus had raised from the dead. They gave a dinner for him there, and Martha served, while Lazarus was one of those reclining at table with

him. Mary took a liter of costly perfumed oil made from genuine aromatic nard and anointed the feet of Jesus and dried them with her hair; the house was filled with the fragrance of the oil.

Martha invited Jesus (and some of his traveling companions) into their home. She immediately began to prepare and serve them dinner. On the other hand, Mary adored Jesus and wanted nothing more than to sit at His feet, be in His presence, and listen to His words and teaching. She also anointed Jesus with expensive oil just days before His passion and crucifixion. What can we learn from these verses about the different personalities and temperaments of these two sisters?

Martha: active, energetic, hospitable, serving, practical, matter of fact, direct, organized, a leader, a planner, loving, caring, concerned, anxious, worried, demanding, impatient.

Mary: devoted, contemplative, reflective, sensitive, respectful, humble, patient, loving, caring, concerned, gentle, generous, kind, charitable, compassionate. Martha might say lazy.

What are your gifts and talents? Most of us have enough self-awareness to realize the personality traits we possess. Are you more like Martha or Mary? Are you a combination of the two? Are you different altogether? There is no "right" answer to these questions because neither Martha nor Mary is the be-all barometer of personality traits or temperament. Understanding the diverse characteristics of these two sisters does help us to get in the right frame of mind to contemplate who we are as designed and conceived by God and blessed by the Holy Spirit to be in the Body of Christ.

Before moving forward with this exercise, I want to distinguish between spiritual and personal gifts. The spiritual gifts of the Holy Spirit include the gift of faith, the seven gifts of the Holy Spirit (wisdom, knowledge, counsel, etc., (Isa. 11:2–3)), and the special graces the apostle Paul wrote about in the verses from Romans 12 and 1 Cor. 12 referenced previously. Spiritual gifts are given at baptism and strengthened at confirmation.

The personal gifts I will discuss here are unique to you, given when you were conceived in your mother's womb. Although some may be inherited, these are your personality and character traits that have and will continue to evolve as you mature. Most likely, these traits will or have already pushed you toward your life vocation.

It is also important to distinguish between personal gifts and talents. While these can and do overlap in some instances, they are different. Talent is often the result of genetics and is strengthened through continual training while the Holy Spirit gives our personal gifts to us. Both are gifts from God and should be used to glorify Him, lead others to Christ, and serve the Church.

Let me explain by sharing what I view to be my gifts and talents. I do so to help get your contemplative juices flowing. Regarding my personal gifts (personality and character traits), I am thoughtful, giving, empathetic, easy-going, considerate, friendly, welcoming, helpful, attentive, goal-oriented, disciplined, and a leader by example.

We should also understand our weaknesses because one person's weaknesses are another person's strengths. I, for one, am not all that organized. Others organize well.

Working together, I can draw on another person's organizational strength, and they can draw on my strengths.

Too often some look down on others because of their weaknesses. Keep this perspective: what may be a struggle for them may be easy for you and what challenges you may come naturally for others. God handpicked our strengths and weaknesses; in His eyes, we are each a masterpiece (Eph. 2:10).

My primary talents are quick wit and a sense of humor, communication skills, and writing. As you consider your talents, please think about your life experiences too because they tend to contribute to our talents.

As part of this personal exploration, it's also helpful to examine our character flaws. Why? Because these will often lead to sinful behavior if not there already. Examples could be laziness, arrogance, dishonesty, anger, and selfishness. By better understanding our faults, we will be more inclined to address and correct them in a way aligned with the will of God. The Holy Spirit will guide us in this examination if we ask for His help.

As we move through this chapter, I'll narrow the list of gifts to the top five to seven that best describe who I am and the best gifts that I bring into the Body of Christ. You will have a chance to narrow your lists too. Later, in Part 3, we will then explore and understand how to best utilize these gifts and talents to glorify God, spread the Gospel message of love, and to bring the light of Christ into the world through the Body of Christ.

> The Lord is also calling you: He is asking you to be a gift wherever you are, just as you are, with everyone around you. Courage! The Lord expects great things from you![5]
> —Pope Francis (@Pontifex)

Now it's time to take an inventory of what you feel are your personal gifts (qualities, personality, abilities, and character traits). There are numerous lists of personality and character traits accessible online. You may choose to look through some of these to help you contemplate your personal gifts. These lists aren't all-inclusive, and there may be other words that describe you; still, you might want to consult them as you take stock of your unique collection of these God-given gifts. Please list as many as you wish below:

_____

_____

_____

_____

How do you feel about this list? Does it represent who you are and how you act? Did you use action words like driven, outspoken, or risk-taking to describe yourself? If you asked friends or family to describe your traits, what words would they use?

Next, list the talents that you have. Remember, a talent is something that you do exceptionally well, something that others might struggle to do, and an ability you have perfected over time with much training and focus. Often, your talent is a result of genetics or physical stature. Your mother may have passed on a talent for singing to you. Your 6'5" height and muscular frame may have allowed you to be exceptional at basketball. You may have had to work hard for years to develop your talent. You may be an expert in your career or vocation. Whatever the case, spend some time listing your talents here:

The Parable of the Talents

Now that we have had an opportunity to contemplate and realize our God-given personal gifts and talents and have written them down, we can turn to the words of Jesus for his teaching and inspiration on what He expects of us in return for God's blessings in our unique characteristics and abilities.

Recall the parable of the talents (Matt. 25:14-30). After entering Jerusalem on Palm Sunday during the last week of his humanity, Jesus taught his disciples:

> For it will be as when a man going on a journey called his servants and entrusted to them his property: to one he gave five talents, to another two, and to another one, to each according to his ability. Then he went away (vv. 14–15).

As the parable continued, Jesus framed up the actions of the three servants. The servant who received five talents invested and returned ten to the master. Likewise, the one who received two talents invested those and made two more, returning double the amount to his master when asked to settle accounts with him. To each of these two diligent servants, Jesus taught:

His master said, "Well done, my good and faithful servant. Since you were faithful in small matters, I will give you great responsibilities. Come, share your master's joy" (vv. 21, 23).

Now the servant who received one talent dug a hole and buried his talent, for he was fearful of his master and only returned the one talent given to him. He did nothing with the responsibility given to him. The master was furious, telling this man:

> "You wicked, lazy servant! So you knew that I harvest where I did not plant and gather where I did not scatter? Should you not then have put my money in the bank so that I could have got it back with interest on my return? Now then! Take the talent from him and give it to the one with ten. For to everyone who has, more will be given and he will grow rich; but from the one who has not, even what he has will be taken away. And throw this useless servant into the darkness outside, where there will be wailing and grinding of teeth" (vv. 26–30).

Quite literally, Christ here states the stakes—that the outcome for the lazy servant is Gehenna.

Turning to the commentaries and notes from a couple of editions of the Bible, we learn a few things about this parable. As it relates to the term talents, the note on Matthew 18:24 (NABRE) tells us, "The talent was a unit of coinage of high but varying value depending on its metal (gold, silver, copper) and its place of origin." In *The Navarre Bible* (RSV-CE), the commentary on Matthew 25:14–30 indicates, "A talent was not any kind of coin but a measure of value worth about thirty-four kilos (seventy-five pounds) of silver." Suffice it to say one talent was of significant value.

In this parable, Jesus contrasts the behavior required to "share your master's joy" in heaven versus being cast "into the darkness outside, where there will be wailing and grinding of teeth." In the New Testament, darkness, outside, and wailing and grinding (gnashing) of teeth mainly refer to exclusion from heaven.

The note on Matthew 25:14 (NABRE) indicates, "Although the comparison is not completed, the sense is clear; the kingdom of heaven is like the situation here described. Faithful use of one's gifts will lead to participation in the fullness of the kingdom, lazy inactivity to exclusion from it."

The commentary on Matt. 25:14-30 referenced previously also offers this: "In this parable our Lord teaches the need to respond to grace by making a genuine effort right through one's life. All the gifts of nature and grace which God has given us should yield a profit. It does not matter how many gifts we have received; what matters is our generosity in putting them to good use: 'You think your life is for yourself? Your life is for God, for the good of all men, through your love for our Lord. Your buried talent, dig it up again!'"[6]

THE EXPECTATION

God has blessed each of us with a different and diverse set of gifts and talents. He expects us to use them to glorify Him and keep Jesus, the head of the Body of Christ, alive in the world. We do this by sharing our gifts and talents with others so they can see Jesus alive in us. We do this by giving ourselves to others. By doing this, we can be filled with

His joy and radiate His love, reflect His light, and exude His Spirit.

He expects us to bring Him a return on His investment in us. He expects us to share these gifts and talents generously. He expects us to put them to good use in the Body of Christ. He expects us to collaborate with other Christians as we feed off each other's strengths and weaknesses to bring this unity into our communities and the world.

To fulfill these divine expectations, it would help to understand and acknowledge our primary gifts and our top talent(s). These are the gifts that best define you. They are the characteristics your close friends and family would use to describe you. Friends see us as we are and can point out things we may overlook or be too humble to include. I encourage asking a friend or family member to participate with you, if possible. In Psalm 145, David tells us more about God than what He shared about Himself on Mount Sinai, saying He also abounds in goodness and is just, compassionate, protective, and trustworthy.

Throughout this process, ask the Holy Spirit to guide you, trust your self-awareness, and make a heartfelt examination of the gifts and talents God has given you.

Drawing from the personal gifts you listed before, narrow that list to your top five to seven. Why seven? For one, the number falls in the range suggested by expert psychologist theories on personality traits. A list of seven gifts will include core or central traits and a couple of strong secondary characteristics that can also emerge in certain situations.[7] Seven [7] is also one of the key recurring numbers in the Bible, symbolizing fulfillment or completeness. I will go first:

My top God-given gifts are: <u>thoughtfulness, empathy, attentiveness, friendliness, helpfulness, a welcoming spirit, and a giving spirit.</u>

My top God-given talents are: <u>having quick-wit, a sense of humor, and good communication skills.</u>

    Now it's your turn. Before you begin to narrow your lists, I want to emphasize something. Wherever you are in your stage of life is where your current gifts and talents will shine. If you are in high school, your gifts and talents may just be emerging; these, and even new ones, will develop further as you mature. What might be your best gifts or talents today may not be your strongest qualities when you enter your work vocation, start to raise a family, or become an empty nester and retire. Do not be concerned that you are limiting yourself in any way by "declaring" what your top gifts and talents are today. You are a child of God and a work in progress, just as is the Body of Christ. Revisiting and recognizing how these might change as your life unfolds is essential.

    Similarly, those who are infirmed, disabled, in assisted living, or elderly and frail may no longer be able to draw upon all the bodily God-given gifts and talents that were strengths when younger or healthier but now can share their wisdom, and kindness and contentment in the face of adversity that makes them a beacon in the Body of Christ. That is the beauty of the cycle of life! You have other gifts and talents in this season of life that you can draw on and shine brightly. You can also receive other people's gifts and talents generously, allowing and helping them to develop those as they play their part at their stage of life.

Jesus will meet you where you are. If you listen and see, the Holy Spirit will enlighten you on how you can best serve others in the Body of Christ.

> There are no barriers for Christians who work together with their Leader Christ, for the good of all. Each one is an important and precious part of the whole. Rich and poor, sick and healthy, young and old, illiterate and genius all work together in the Divine Presence which dwells in each one as in a living Temple.[8]
> —Mother Angelica, *Jesus Needs Me*

Please list your best five to seven God-given gifts and your best two or three talents below.

My top God-given gifts are: _____

_____

My top God-given talents are: _____

_____

I will conclude this chapter with a few thought-provoking quotes.

> Creativity is not a mood. Creativity is not a gift. It is the very nature of God inside of you.
> —Unknown

> You may try any path you wish. You may try to find yourself in a thousand different ways, but in a wonderfully profound and mysterious way, it is only through self-donation–giving ourselves to others–that we discover our true self.[9]
> —Matthew Kelly, *Amazing Possibilities*

What we have received, we must pass on and not pocket; what has been given to us must not be confined, but cradled for growth. As guardians of the Divine Life which has come down to us since Pentecost, we must answer to God for misappropriation and impounding His gifts to our own ends. Every talent received must bear interest.[10]
—Fulton J. Sheen, *The Mystical Body of Christ*

Now that you have spent some time realizing how God has blessed you with unique gifts and talents, it is time to think about how God wants you to use them. The next chapter will enlighten and help you become more attuned to what God has in store for you and what His plan is for you in the Body of Christ. It will help you better concentrate on if your free will conforms to the will of the Father and it will lead you down the path toward your destiny.

5
DESTINY

For we are his handiwork, created in Christ Jesus for the
good works that God has prepared in advance,
that we should live in them.
—Ephesians 2:10

It is natural for us to wish that God had designed for us a less
glorious and less arduous destiny; but then we are
wishing not for more love but for less.
—C.S. Lewis *A Mind Awake: An Anthology of C.S. Lewis*

The blood cells serve a unique function in the human body, sent
out by the heart for a specific purpose and returning to the heart
to replenish nutrients before being sent again.
—Marty Mitchell

Most of us wake up each day with to-do lists, objectives, or responsibilities that shape our plans for the day. You know what they say about our "best-laid plans." Things don't always go according to our plans. Perhaps you have heard the quip "We plan, and God smiles."

Like me, I'm sure you can remember many times when your day didn't follow your intended plan. You got a flat tire on your way to work, and a passerby, out of the kindness of his heart, stopped to help. You came upon the scene of an accident, and your conscience led you to stop to give aid to the victims, missing your appointment. Your child needed you, delaying your weekend morning plans. Your dear friend phoned to tell you about some good news in her life, leading you to be patient, holding off on your plans so you could share in her happiness and success. Unexpected traffic caused you to be late for the meeting.

Were all these occurrences just happenstance? Maybe, although I believe they happened for a good reason and by the grace of God. The instances of the flat tire and the traffic may have prevented you from being involved in the accident that occurred up ahead had you not been delayed. Your flat tire allowed that passerby to be a Good Samaritan. What led you to aid the victims of the accident was the Holy Spirit working in your conscience to share the love of God with those in need at that time. Your concern for your child allowed you to emulate the Holy Family. Sharing the success and happiness of your dear friend without envy and at the expense of your plans is what Christians are called to do in the Body of Christ.

Bishop Robert Barron of the Diocese of Winona-Rochester (Minnesota), an author, speaker, theologian, and the founder of global media ministry Word on Fire, offers this perspective on the faith and trust that guides so many as they set out on their daily travels.

> Faith is an attitude of trust in the presence of God. Faith is an openness to what God will reveal, do, and invite.

It should be obvious that in dealing with the infinite, all-powerful person who is God, we are never in control.

One of the most fundamental statements of faith is this: your life is not about you. You're not in control. This is not your project. Rather, you are part of God's great design.[1]

Choices and Free Will

God has a plan and purpose for each of us. He first conceived of us before being conceived in our mother's womb. Recalling what the Lord said to the prophet Jeremiah, "before I formed you in the womb, I knew you, before you were born I dedicated you, a prophet to the nations I appointed you" (Jer. 1:5). He also told him "For I know well the plans I have in mind for you" (Jer. 29:11).

Now, very few of us were dedicated and appointed to be a prophet to the nations before we were born. Our lives were conceived by God, though, and He blessed us with gifts, talents, time, and treasure, intending that we live according to His will in the world and as the Body of Christ. Whether we follow His will or allow evil impulses to lead us astray is our choice. Our free will determines the choice we make.

Although God is in control, He has given us the freedom to choose between good and evil, "and thus of growing in perfection or of failing and sinning" (CCC 1732). God has also "created [the human] a rational being, conferring on [them] the dignity of a person who can initiate and control [their] own actions" (CCC 1730).

For you were called for freedom, brothers. But do not use this freedom as an opportunity for the flesh; rather, serve one another through love.
—Galatians 5:13

Every time we give in to selfishness and say "No" to God, we spoil his loving plan for us.[2]
—Pope Francis (@Pontifex)

GOD'S PLAN—THE PATH OF LOVE

Our free will aligns with the will of God when we are on the path of love. Bishop Barron tells us, "Broadly speaking, what God wants is the path for you of greatest love."[3] What is love? First and foremost, God is love (1 John 4:8,16). Love is who, what, and how God is. How are we to love like God? Drawing from St. Thomas Aquinas' definition of love, Bishop Barron also said, "to love is to will the good of the other, as other."[4] In other words, love is willing the good of others without expectation of anything in return. Love is self-giving, sacrificial, inconveniencing, and selfless.

At the Last Supper, Jesus said:

I give you a new commandment: love one another. As I have loved you, so you also should love one another. This is how all will know that you are my disciples, if you have love for one another.
—John 13:34-35

Popular verses from the Bible tell us love is loving your neighbor just as you love yourself. Love is doing to others as you want them to do to you. Love is loving the least of our brothers and sisters, the oppressed, and those at the fringes of society. To love God is to spread His love to the ends of the earth, to the extremities of the Body of Christ.

The notes from 1 John 4:13-21 (NABRE) teach, "Christian love is not abstract but lived in the concrete manner of love for one another." Bishop Barron echoed this when he preached, "to love is really to want what is advantageous to another person and to act concretely on that desire."[5] Love is not only a desire for what is in the best interest of another person, it requires action.

> Christian love always possesses one quality: concreteness. Christian love is concrete. Jesus himself, when he speaks of love, tells us concrete things: feed the hungry, visit the sick.[6]
>
> —Pope Francis

We are on a unique path in this life and a unique spiritual journey. No two are the same. Drawing from our experiences, we each have so much to share. God has a unique plan and purpose for each of us, a unique part to play in His Body. The part chosen for you will allow you to share best the love of God that is deep in your soul with others and to bring the face and light of Jesus into the world. The part you are to play is the one that will allow you to bring charity to those who need it most, right now, in the present moment. The part you are to play is the one that will let others come to know Jesus through your actions, your words, your touch, and your love.

We are each responsible for the choices that we make, of course. For example, God doesn't necessarily preordain the professions that we choose. He blesses us with gifts and talents that may lead us in a particular direction. However, He allows us to make decisions throughout every day. When these choices vary from the path He has prepared for us, He steers us back on course through new circumstances, relationships, and opportunities.

We need to ask God to open our eyes to see where He is leading us and to help us listen to Him with the ear of our hearts. He speaks to us and guides us in so many ways and at just the right time: in prayer, a new friend, a bible verse, a quote, a bumper sticker, an interaction, an opportunity to help a stranger, an opportunity to receive help from a neighbor, and a gentle nudge from His still, small voice through the Holy Spirit (1 Kings 19:11-13). I could go on and on with many ways God leads, guides, and speaks to us. All He wants for us is to see, listen, and respond to His promptings with love, faith, and trust.

> God isn't limited by what you think you can do for him. He has dreams for you that surpass your expectations. Just keep coming to him every day, and ask him to guide you. Over time, your path will become clear.[7]
> —*The Word Among Us*

What is your destiny while in this life on Earth? What insight can we gain from the Gospel about the guidance Jesus gives us? We know we are called to love.

Jesus also calls us to bear fruit in the world. To understand this, we return to Jesus' allegory about the vine and the branches. This teaching will also help us perceive what it means to do the will of God. Jesus said this to His disciples:

> I am the true vine, and my Father is the vine grower. He takes away every branch in me that does not bear fruit,

and every one that does he prunes so that it bears more fruit. You are already pruned because of the word that I spoke to you. Remain in me, as I remain in you. Just as a branch cannot bear fruit on its own unless it remains on the vine, so neither can you unless you remain in me. I am the vine, you are the branches. Whoever remains in me and I in him will bear much fruit, because without me you can do nothing.

—John 15:1-5

Jesus says God the Father is the vine grower who tends to the vine, who is Jesus. We, all baptized Christians, are the branches that must remain in (attached to) the vine (Jesus) to bear good fruit in the Body of Christ. Those who remain in Jesus and bear fruit are "pruned" by the Father to grow stronger and bear *more* fruit. The pruning process may involve loving discipline when we stray, bringing our free will in line with the Father's will by closing one unfruitful door and opening a fruitful one, correcting a character flaw, and other measures He deems necessary for our sanctification. The pruning process can sometimes be difficult and painful, some more than others. We need to increase in trust and hope, knowing that God loves us unconditionally and wants what is best for us.

The visual Jesus presents here is so very instructive. To tie it into the Body of Christ, it also helps to visualize the human circulatory system. The similarities to the vine and branches are pretty remarkable:

- The primary artery in the human body is the aorta—resembling *the vine*.
- Smaller arteries and tiny capillaries extend from the aorta—or *branch* out from *the vine*.

- These arterial *branches bear fruit* by transporting oxygen-rich blood filled with other nutrients from the heart to other parts of the body. They are *pruned* to become stronger by exercise and clean and healthy living so they can *bear more fruit*, just as the healthy, fruitful branches (faithful Christians) attached to the vine get *pruned* by *the word* of God to strengthen them so they can *bear more fruit*.
- If one of these blood vessels (branches) fails to function (bear fruit) or gets clogged (by infection, or sin), it fails to *remain on the vine* (remain attached to Jesus). These, the Father *takes away* (bypassed surgically) because *"a branch cannot bear fruit on its own unless it remains on the vine."* Without Jesus, the vine, *"you can do nothing."*

*(Words in italics are from verse above.)

Now back to the meaning of the words of Jesus. How do we bear this fruit? St. Paul urges us "to live in a manner worthy of the call you have received, with all humility and gentleness, with patience, bearing with one another through love" (Eph. 4:1–2). We bear fruit by being attentive and saying yes to God at each opportunity. In opposition, we are "taken away" from the vine and from God's plan for us by selfishness that leads to sin, causing us to say no to His will and disobey His commandments.

We bear fruit when we remain in Jesus and abide in and grow in His love, when we allow His word to remain in us, when we are open to and carry out God's will, and when we love God with all our being, love our neighbor as we love ourselves, and love one another as Jesus loves us.

To bear fruit, we need to share and invest the unique God-given gifts and talents we listed in Chapter 4 in concrete and tangible ways with those we encounter daily (more on this in Chapter 11). We should do so not boastfully or self-enrichingly but with the intention of glorifying God and in the name of Jesus Christ.

For Christians, this means always being attentive to those around us and lending a helping hand to someone who might need it in the present moment. Someone with empathy could stop to help the elderly shopper at the grocery store who is having difficulty reaching something off the top shelf. If you have thoughtfulness, you could slow down on a busy highway to allow that person to move in front of you who is struggling to get into the exit lane. The introvert might offer a smile and a prayer for a homeless person she passes on the sidewalk. A strong leader could take control of a sudden evacuation effort. You could send a thoughtful text encouraging a friend before a stiff competition. When we do these things, we glorify God, bring the light and face of Jesus to those around us, and spread the love of the Holy Trinity through the Body of Christ.

Jesus offers a summation of the allegory of the vine and branches in these verses:

> By this is my Father glorified, that you bear much fruit and become my disciples. As the Father loves me, so I also love you. Remain in my love. If you keep my commandments, you will remain in my love, just as I have kept my Father's commandments and remain in his love.
>
> It was not you who chose me, but I who chose you and appointed you to go and bear fruit that will remain, so that whatever you ask the Father in my name he may give you. This I command you: love one another.
> —John 15:8–10,16-17

Your eternal destiny is the kingdom of God in heaven. You live your destiny here on Earth as you play your part in the Body of Christ. Back to our analogy, the permeable nature of the capillaries in the human body allows for an exchange to occur in the body tissue where oxygen and nutrients exit the vessels and carbon dioxide and waste enter them. You and I are called to be a channel of our Lord's peace, love, joy, and mercy – a permeable channel where these qualities pour out of our hearts into others (regardless of whether they are part of the Body of Christ) and return to us immeasurably. In the words of St. Francis of Assisi, "for it is in giving that we receive."

In one of his *Daily Gospel Reflections* (2018), Bishop Barron wrote, "the tree that bears no fruit is evocative of the moral person who bears no spiritual fruit. Every single person has a mission: to be a conduit of the divine grace in the world."[8] Now that Jesus has returned to heaven, His mission has become our mission. We are His ambassadors. Another quote from Bishop Barron is right on point too. "When our lives are aligned to God we become conduits of enormous power."[9]

When you use God's gifts and talents in this manner, you become intriguing to others, exude His Spirit, radiate His love, reflect His light, attract others to Jesus, and build up His Body.

Resist feeling overwhelmed or anxious about it. Trust, and just get started. Take the first step and listen for the Holy Spirit because He will guide you from there. Allow God "to produce what effects He wills, and when He wills, from the hopes we have and the efforts we make."[10]

DESTINY

Be who God meant you to be and you will set the world on fire.[11]

—St. Catherine of Siena

Matthew Kelly of Dynamic Catholic offers this perspective on St. Catherine's quote: it "rightly points out that there are natural consequences for the whole world when we find and live out our mission in life. When we are faithful to who God created us to be, and what God calls us to do, incredible things happen."[12]

The great thing is your potential reaches to heaven and back! The next chapter will help you understand how fully equipped you are to live your destiny in the Body of Christ. How? By igniting the fire that is already deep inside you.

6
POTENTIAL

I ask you to consider that our Lord Jesus Christ is your true head and that you are a member of his body. He belongs to you as the head belongs to the body. All that is his is yours: breath, heart, soul and all his faculties. All of these you must use as if they belonged to you, so that in serving him you may give him praise, love and glory.
—St. John Eudes

Give yourself to God. He will use you to accomplish great things on the condition that you believe much more in His love than in your own weakness.
—St. Teresa of Calcutta

The human heart beats approximately 2.5 billion times in the life span of a 75-year-old person.

Joan of Arc was an 18-year-old maid with no military training. Believing she received guidance from God through St. Michael and other saints, she became the national heroine of France after leading the French army to victory in battle against an attempt to conquer her homeland by the English during a phase of the Hundred Years' War in the early 1400s.

Francis of Assisi was born into an affluent family, was popular in his youth, and, growing up, was regarded as a leader among his peers. As he matured, he became restless and spent time in silence, prayer, and intentional poverty, attempting to discern God's will. Later while praying in front of the crucifix, he heard Jesus say, "Rebuild my Church. Which is falling into ruin."

Initially thinking Jesus meant for him to repair the physical walls of the church, he restored a few chapels and churches, ultimately realizing the Church Jesus wanted him to rebuild was, effectively, the Body of Christ.

After leaving his family, renouncing the things of the world, and pledging a life of poverty in his early twenties, he spent the rest of his life preaching the Gospel, developing a deep love for nature and animals, and establishing several religious orders that are still instrumental in the Church today.

In the twenty-first century, four fictional good friends from the same church led ordinary lives by modern societal standards. They didn't lead an army into battle, take a pledge of poverty, or establish a religious order. They simply loved God and their neighbor and did little things every day that brought the light and face of Jesus to those around them. It may have been a smile here, a helping hand there, or a prayer for a struggling stranger who crossed their path during their day.

Joan of Arc and Francis of Assisi took giant leaps of faith, listened intently to the divine messages they were receiving, stepped out of their comfort zones, and took action according to God's will. They trusted the plan God had for them and, by His grace, faced any fear or adversity that may have gotten in their way. By loving and listening intently to God, they carried out His mission for them and became Saints beloved by Christians worldwide.

The four fictional friends represent you, me, and all Christians in the Body of Christ. When we become increasingly aware of God's presence in our lives, break through all the worldly distractions, listen intently to Him, and see the face of Jesus in others, we can also respond to our saintly calling. It doesn't need to be monumental either, although God will give greater callings to some at points in life. The little things we do daily are equally as important when done with love because it allows us to act as the hands and feet of Jesus in His Body and throughout the world.

The people mentioned in the paragraphs above had unique gifts and talents, and they leapt onto the path God had planned for them. They were each fully equipped to respond to the voice of God in their lives, whether it was to perform heroic acts, humble themselves for God's greater glory, or be a small miracle to those they encountered in their community daily.

No matter how grand their deed or the time they endured to do it, each person rose to their potential at the right time to play their part in the Body of Christ. How? By listening for the Father's will for them through Jesus Christ and acting in unity with the Holy Spirit.

We have immense potential to fulfill the part Jesus wants us to play in His Body. That potential emanates from our hearts and souls, "the nest of love" (St. [Padre] Pio of Pietrelcina prayer, "Stay With Me, Lord") where the Holy Spirit resides. The same Spirit is the soul of the Body of

Christ, flowing from the Head (Jesus) into the body (CCC 782). We are anointed with the Holy Spirit at baptism, and the Holy Spirit is strengthened in us at confirmation. Fr. Michael Van Sloun of the Archdiocese of St. Paul and Minneapolis wrote, "Confirmation is not the new arrival of the Holy Spirit, but rather an intensification of the presence and power of the Holy Spirit."[1]

Fr. Van Sloun also wrote, "All who are confirmed are equipped with the gifts of the Holy Spirit to live a virtuous and holy life and sent forth to bear much fruit, . . . The graces of the Spirit strengthen confirmed Christians to carry out their vocations for the good of others and the benefit of the Church and the world."[2]

Every Christian is a temple of the Holy Spirit (1 Cor. 6:19). What a gift this is! Ponder this for a moment. We stand on hallowed ground. We usher the Spirit everywhere we go and encounter the Holy Spirit when interacting with other Christians. However, St. Paul warned, "Do you not know that you are the temple of God, and that the Spirit of God dwells in you? If anyone destroys God's temple, God will destroy that person; for the temple of God, which you are, is holy" (1 Cor. 3:16–17).

It is a tremendous responsibility to protect this temple from sin and evil. St. Lucy of Rome echoed St. Paul's sentiment that all Christians may not be worthy temples of the Spirit when she said, "Those whose hearts are pure are temples of the Holy Spirit." Jesus said Himself, "blessed are the pure in heart" (Matt. 5:8). Bishop Barron says when we are single-hearted, desiring only to please God, we are pure in heart (Sunday homily January 29, 2023). The purer our hearts, the greater our potential.

The presence and the power of the Holy Spirit live in us. Christians believe the Holy Spirit is the third person of the Holy Trinity. Three persons, one God – the Father, the Son, and the Holy Spirit. The Holy Spirit, the Lord, the giver of life, proceeds from the Father and the Son (Nicene Creed). Jesus lives in us in the person of the Holy Spirit.

Bishop Barron offers excellent insight into this relationship. He has said the Holy Spirit is the "sigh of love" between the Father and the Son. According to Barron, the Spirit is the love that binds the Father and the Son together. The Holy Spirit has many names and titles. Some of those listed here are **biblical**; others come from our experiences. Praying on and contemplating these will help us to get to know and understand the Holy Spirit more fully. The Holy Spirit is:

The living water
Our Advocate (counselor, helper)
Our comforter
Our consoler
Our divine guidance
Spirit of love
Spirit of truth
Spirit of promise
Spirit of faith
Spirit of faithfulness
Spirit of understanding
Spirit of wisdom
Spirit of devotion
Spirit of commitment
Spirit of hope
Spirit of hopefulness
Spirit of counsel
Spirit of fortitude (courage/strength)

Spirit of knowledge
Spirit of piety (authentic religious spirit, childlike confidence)
Spirit of reverence/awe (fear of the Lord)
Spirit of contrition
Spirit of mercy
Spirit of peace
Spirit of gentleness
Spirit of prayer

And He is closer to us than the air we breathe.

Think about it. The Holy Spirit takes up residence in our hearts and souls. Any feeling or inkling that moves us toward love, peace, faith, devotion, understanding, courage to act, etc., is initiated in us by the Holy Spirit. It is not we who invite God into prayer. Our desire to pray is always initiated by God in the Holy Spirit! (CCC 2560, 2567) In 1 Corinthians 12:3, St. Paul said, "And no one can say 'Jesus is Lord,' except by the Holy Spirit."

The presence and the power of the Holy Spirit live in us. And yes, He is closer to us than the air that we breathe. To get a feel for this, part your lips for a second. Now slowly and gently inhale through your parted lips. Feel the air cascade past your lips and touch your tongue. Now contemplate that the Holy Spirit is infinitely closer to and alive in you. He is the oxygen of our faith.

The Holy Spirit descended from the heavens and came upon Jesus at His baptism (Matt. 3:16). He led Jesus into the desert for forty days (Matt. 4:1–2) to prepare Him to reach His potential in the three-year ministry that took Him to the cross at Calvary. The breath and fire of the Holy Spirit descended on the apostles at Pentecost and filled them up (Acts 2:4) to enable them to reach their potential in spreading the Good News and building the Church. The

Holy Spirit has filled up Christians through the centuries since the resurrection to enable them to reach their potential in playing their part in the Body of Christ.

Although the Holy Spirit resides in us, He is only as effective in putting us on the path of love as we allow Him to be. Our hearts must be open to listening to, understanding, and acting upon the promptings of the Holy Spirit. Our hearts must be pure and not entirely distracted by worldly things. We must also acknowledge our need for His guidance, direction, and love by inviting Him into our souls, hearts, and minds and asking Him to move in us and to work through us.

One way to do this is simply praying. "Come, Holy Spirit." This short prayer has invoked the Holy Spirit since ancient times. It is a prayer that gives me great peace. I sometimes call on Him throughout the day to help with decisions I need to make, before conversations, before responding in conversation, to calm my mind, to help me listen, and to guide me in prayer, in my thoughts and feelings, in my words and actions, and when I need help discerning God's will. I repeatedly pray this short prayer while writing this book, asking the Holy Spirit to bless me with His wisdom.

When we invite the Holy Spirit into our hearts, souls, and minds, His fire is ignited within us just as it was in the disciples on Pentecost and just as it has been in ordinary people who lived saintly lives down through the ages.

The Holy Spirit is readily available to fill us with the confidence to step forward in faith, with the boldness to express our faith and the conviction to stand up for what we believe, with the willingness to speak out for justice, and with the compassion and desire to share the love of God with others.

Extending the prayer, it reads "Come Holy Spirit, fill the hearts of your faithful and enkindle in them the fire of your love."

> Your life is not about you. It's about what the Holy Spirit wants to accomplish through you."[3]
>
> —Bishop Robert Barron

> God himself is the source of all love. And you have that source to draw from dwelling within you – the Holy Spirit. So be encouraged: loving is up to you. But it's not all up to you![4]
>
> —*The Word Among Us*

When graced with the willingness to have the Holy Spirit work through us and we work in concert with the Holy Spirit, we become unstoppable.

You have now had a chance to contemplate the Holy Spirit and to realize that the presence and the power of the Holy Spirit in you ensure that you are fully equipped to play your part in the Body of Christ. The next chapter will highlight how all Christians are unified in the Body of Christ to carry out the mission of the People of God.

7
UNIFIED

Rather, living the truth in love, we should grow in every way into him who is the head, Christ, from whom the whole body, joined and held together by every supporting ligament, with the proper functioning of each part, brings about the body's growth and builds itself up in love.
—Ephesians 4:15–16

Build for your team a feeling of oneness, of dependence on one another and of strength to be derived by unity.
—Vince Lombardi

The human body never loses the ability to grow new blood vessels. The vessels are constructed throughout the body, then join together to form the whole circulatory system.[1]
—Heart Matters Magazine

As I write, today is Monday, January 18. The significance of this date is it is the first day of the annual International Week of Prayer for Christian Unity. It just so happens I am sitting down to begin writing this next chapter designed to help all members of the Body of Christ recognize we are unified in our calling to bring the light, face, and Good News of Jesus into the world. The writing herein is offered as a prayer for Christian unity. I invite you to pause here and pray for Christian unity.

Was the timing of this intentional? No, it was not. I finished the previous chapter last week and am returning to it after a weekend break. Coincidence? Possibly. Or perhaps, might I be so bold as to suggest, it could be the hand of Jesus reaching out from His Last Supper prayer to the Father:

> And I have given them the glory you gave me, so that they may all be one, as we are one, I in them and you in me, that they may be brought to perfection as one.
> —John 17:22–23

Considering the timing and purpose of this chapter, I would be remiss if I did not touch on the efforts toward Christian unity. The message of this book is love and Christian unity. I hope that readers will be reminded that one of the deep desires of Jesus is to see all Christian believers united as one. By the grace of God, our Christian leaders have made strides toward healing the divisions between Catholics, Orthodox, and Protestants in the last 50 years, yet there is still much work to be done.

For one, some non-Catholic Christians still do not believe or are unaware that those of us in the Catholic faith are Christian. The founder of what became the Roman Catholic Church was Jesus Christ Himself—"And so I say to you, you are Peter, and upon this rock I will build my church" (Matt. 16:18). For the first 1000 years after Pentecost until the Great Schism in 1054 (when the faction that became the Eastern Orthodox separated from the

Roman Catholic Church) it was the only Christian Church. Catholics are Christian followers of Jesus Christ and all His teachings.

> So also I cannot call myself by any other name than what I am—a Christian.
>
> —St. Perpetua

There are doctrinal differences that indeed must resolve, although progress is being made. Catholic, Methodist, Lutheran, Anglican, and Reformed leaders have agreed on and issued a *Joint Declaration on the Doctrine of Justification*.[2] The relations between Orthodox and Catholic leaders have warmed, and there have been discussions on the role of the papacy. Pope St. John Paul II made Christian unity a priority in his pontificate. With great humility, he came to a much better understanding of and appreciation for the Eastern Orthodox church's gifts for all of Christianity.[3]

While there remain disagreements on the important doctrines of the Real Presence in the Eucharist, the role of Mary, the papacy, apostolic succession, purgatory, and others, there is more that unites all Christians: the sacrament of baptism, the Trinitarian God, the Scriptures, the Nicene Creed, salvation in Jesus Christ, the divinity of Christ, the gift of the Holy Spirit, and the hope of eternal life in heaven.

So, while the leaders of the Catholic Church, the Orthodox, and the mainline Protestant denominations, together with others who have ecumenical (promoting and seeking unity) responsibilities around the world, work toward solving the doctrinal divisions, let us, brothers and sisters in Christ and privileged members of the Body of Christ, focus instead on what unites us. Let us work together in a way that magnifies our unified Christian beliefs, gives encouragement and courage to our leaders to break down the barriers that separate us, and glorifies God through Jesus Christ. From *The Word Among Us* "The answer to divisions, whether big or small, is Jesus. It's simple but true."[4]

> For whatever was written previously was written for our instruction, that by endurance and by the encouragement of the scriptures we might have hope. May the God of endurance and encouragement grant you to think in harmony with one another, in keeping with Christ Jesus, that with one accord you may with one voice glorify the God and Father of our Lord Jesus Christ.
> —Romans 15:4–6

> Christian Unity—we are convinced—will not be the fruit of subtle theoretical discussions.… When the Son of Man comes, he will find us still discussing! . . . We need to encounter one another and to challenge one another under the guidance of the Holy Spirit, who harmonizes diversities, overcomes conflicts, reconciles differences.[5]
> —Pope Francis

I will now transition from discussing the status of Christian unity to highlighting how well-unified the members of the Body of Christ are with one another. By the grace of God, once we can grasp and accept this, we will consciously grow in our solidarity with each other, and we will become more aware of opportunities to cooperate as we all seek to play our part in the Body of Christ.

So He, the glorified Christ in heaven, seeks the enlistment of you and me—all of us—under his headship.[6]
—Fulton J. Sheen

How are we unified? All Christians share an abundance of beauty and greatness in Christianity. I listed some of these above and will go into more detail here.

We are unified by our baptism with water in the name of the Father, and of the Son, and of the Holy Spirit. All Christians who receive a valid baptism "have put on Christ" (Gal. 3:27), been "born of water and Spirit" (John 3:5), and have been anointed by and blessed with the gift of the same Holy Spirit. This is important, for without the anointing of the Holy Spirit, we are individuals; with the Spirit, we are unified as one.

We are unified because of the certain, although imperfect, communion in the Church, the Body of Christ. "The Church knows that she is joined in many ways to the baptized who are honored by the name of Christian, but do not profess the Catholic faith in its entirety or have not preserved unity or communion under the successor of Peter" (*Lumen Gentium* #15).

Recall Bishop Sheen's succinct description of the Church as "A body animated by a living soul – the Spirit of God."[7] Not only is the Church brought to life by the Holy Spirit, but all Christians have also had life breathed into them by "the Holy Spirit, the Lord, the giver of life" (Nicene Creed). The beating heart in the human body is mission-critical. Without it, blood doesn't circulate, and the body dies. The Holy Spirit is the heart and soul of the Church and is mission-critical for every member of the Body of Christ. Without the presence of the Holy Spirit, our souls would die. With the Holy Spirit, our souls are alive, and our souls are immortal. We are unified by our souls.

We are unified because we are the People of God. "One becomes a member of this people not by physical birth, but by being 'born anew,' a birth 'of water and the Spirit,' that is, by faith in Christ, and Baptism" (CCC 782). We are unified by our faith in Jesus Christ as our Lord and Savior and our profession of faith in the Nicene Creed.

We are unified because God created all humans in His image and likeness. God is love. In His image and likeness, we are drawn toward love and to doing good. Pope Francis said in his homily at his daily Mass on May 22, 2013, "we are the image of the Lord, and he does good and all of us have this commandment at heart: do good and avoid evil. All of us."[8] This is not exclusive to Christians either.

We are unified by the new and greatest commandments of love spoken by Jesus to "love the Lord your God with all your heart, with all your soul, with all your mind, and with all your strength" and to "love your neighbor as yourself" (Mark 12:30–31). We are united in this charity.

We are unified in and by our prayer to God the Father through Jesus Christ in the unity of the Holy Spirit. Oh, how prayer unites us! How much more unified can a people be than by offering prayers of intercession for each other or in unity for a greater cause?

We are unified because Jesus has redeemed all mankind, all of humanity through the end of time. In his homily, Pope Francis also said "The Lord has redeemed all of us, all of us, with the Blood of Christ: all of us, not just Catholics. Everyone. Even the atheists. Everyone."[9] In His good shepherd discourse, the notes on John 10:16 say Jesus indicates, "his mission extends to all mankind, for he calls all God's children to enter his Church" (University of Navarre, The Navarre Bible 2001, 261). Regrettably, some do not accept the invitation and lose the hope of salvation.

> I am the good shepherd, and I know mine and mine know me, just as the Father knows me and I know the Father; and I will lay down my life for my sheep. I have other sheep that do not belong to this fold. These also I must lead, and they will hear my voice, and there will be one flock, one shepherd.
>
> —John 10:14–16

Furthermore, Catholics, Orthodox, and the various Protestant denominations also have traditions that may unify those members even more. For example, the sacred Traditions in the Catholic Church that further unite the 1.3 billion Catholics in the world today[10] are the Real Presence in the Holy Eucharist, the order and liturgy of the Mass, the seven sacraments, the Blessed Mother, the communion of saints, the canonization of saints, Sacred Scripture, the papacy, and apostolic succession of the Church, among others.

We are living in the Age of the Holy Spirit—the time between the Resurrection of Jesus on the first Easter and His second coming, or His *Parousia* (arrival in ancient Greek). The same Holy Spirit who "came upon" the Virgin Mary to conceive Jesus at the annunciation (Luke 1:34-35) is the same Holy Spirit who descended like a dove and came upon Jesus at His baptism (Matt. 3:16), is the same Holy Spirit who was breathed by Jesus on the disciples in the Upper Room on the day of His resurrection (John 20:22), is the same Holy Spirit who descended on and filled up the apostles, the Blessed Mother, and other disciples on Pentecost, and is the same Holy Spirit who has anointed and filled every Christian at their baptism from Pentecost to the present day.

More than anything, we are all unified because the same Holy Spirit lives in each of us. This is the same Holy Spirit who has anointed Christians in Biloxi, Boston, Louisville, Little Rock, Rapid City, Reno, and Santa Barbara. The same Holy Spirit dwells in Christians throughout the Americas, Africa, Asia, Europe, Australia, and Antarctica. The same Holy Spirit lives in Christians in the furthest-reaching corners of the world.

This is the same Holy Spirit who, because He is the heart and soul of the Church, is the heart and soul of the Body of Christ. Pope Pius XII wrote, "All the parts of the body are joined one with the other and with their exalted head; for the whole Spirit of Christ is in the head, the whole Spirit is in the body, and the whole Spirit is in each of the members."[11]

He is the identical Holy Spirit who lives in all People of God: the poor, the infirmed, the suffering, the imprisoned, the destitute, the mentally ill, the physically and emotionally unable, the hungry, the thirsty, the homeless, the downtrodden, the depressed, the anxious, the naked, the humble, the unemployed, the desperate, the beggar, the lonely, the alone, the crying, the grieving, the spiritually lost, the fallen away, the sinner, the angry, the abused, the hurting, the elderly, the detached, the broken-hearted, the lost, the addicted, the broken, the despairing, the stranger, the blind, the deaf, the successful, the confident, the joyful, the faithful, the trusting, the hospitable, the satisfied, the content, the wealthy, the comfortable, the healthy, the peaceful, the kind, the concerned, and the compassionate.

Regardless of our state or circumstances, we are always unified by the Holy Spirit who lives in our hearts and souls.

By the power of the Holy Spirit, amazing things happen: the inspiration of the prophets, the conception of Jesus in the Virgin Mary, the baptism of Jesus, the resurrection, the ascension into heaven, the spawning of the early Church, the actions and missionary work of the apostles and their successors in teaching sacred Tradition, the writing of the Gospels and other books of the Holy Bible, the protection of Sacred Scripture and the translation of the Bible down through the generations, communion of the faithful with Jesus Christ in the sacramental liturgy of the Eucharist, the sanctification of the saints, and the inspiration for and intercession in our prayers.

United by the Holy Spirit, all baptized Christians are called to keep Jesus alive in the Body of Christ. In my opinion, Fulton Sheen wrote it best:

> Christ in His Life in the Church has no other hands with which to give bread to the poor than our hands; He has no other feet with which to visit the sick than our feet; He has no other lips with which to speak truth than our lips; He is therefore *incomplete* [italics in the original] without us, in the sense that St. Paul says the Church is "His fullness."[12]

The Holy Spirit continues to work through each of us, omnipresent (everywhere simultaneously) in the world and guiding the hands, feet, and lips of the members of the Body of Christ every minute around the clock in more ways than we will ever know. When we realize the Holy Spirit is at the core of our commonality and the core of our unified calling in the Body of Christ, we become obliged to strive to put our differences aside and to come together to spread the Good News through our words and actions and to keep the light of Christ alive in the world. The apostle Paul said in Ephesians 4:2–6 that we should bear with "one another through love, striving to preserve the unity of the spirit through the bond of peace: one body and one Spirit."

Mother Angelica, Foundress of The Eternal Word Television Network (EWTN), wrote, "Every Christian is 'a letter from Christ' to the world, 'written not with ink, but with the Spirit of the living God,' written, 'not on stone tablets but in their living hearts.'"[13] Bishop Barron put it this way in one of his *Daily Gospel Reflections* "many Christians think of their spiritual lives in an individualist way, as the cultivation of their personal friendship with God. But this overlooks something that the New Testament authors took for granted—namely, that Christians exist not for themselves but for the world."[14]

> All of us who have received one and the same spirit, that is, the Holy Spirit, are in a sense blended together with one another and with God.[15]
> —St. Cyril of Alexandria

Up to this point, you have had a chance to understand the Body of Christ from a biblical perspective with the symbolic help of the human circulatory system. You have also been able to contemplate these things: you are uniquely endowed by God, He has a plan just for you, and you are capable of reaching your earthly destiny, as well as how well-equipped you are to play your part in the Body of Christ and how unified you are with all Christians on this journey.

It's now time to help you understand how to put what was conveyed in Part 1: Creation and discovered in Part 2: Contemplation into practice in your life. The following section, Part 3: Cultivation, will offer practical and relatable ideas, examples, and suggestions of the opportunities surrounding you to play your part and will open your mind to the possibilities to fulfill your calling to keep Jesus alive in the world.

PART 3

Cultivation

But those sown on rich soil are the ones who hear the word and accept it and bear fruit thirty and sixty and a hundredfold.
—Mark 4:20

If there were no God, there would be no atheists.
—G.K. Chesterton

Human blood cells are made in the bone marrow, starting as young parent stem cells that can grow into red blood cells, white blood cells, or platelets.

8
NUTRIENTS

So whether you eat or drink, or whatever you do,
do everything for the glory of God.
—1 Corinthians 10:31

The vast expanse of the capillary bed allows the blood to
transport oxygen and nutrients to every cell in the
body and to carry carbon dioxide and waste away
from every extremity.

My former in-laws bought their first farm in the 1950s on 156 acres in their home state on the east coast. Suddenly, without a lot of experience, they were vegetable and grain farmers. Along with that came the responsibility of caring for and cultivating the soil and the land. They learned as they went along and grew the operation to where over 13,000 acres were being farmed by 2000.

Cultivating for a farmer requires removing weeds and loosening the land to break up the hard and crusty surface and facilitate the penetration and retention of air, water, and nutrients into the soil. The roots of the plants will then have plentiful access to these essential ingredients, resulting in a healthy harvest and strong crop yields.

The use of cover crops in fall and winter adds nutrients to the soil. In addition, crop rotation (in the same field) is also vital to keep the land fertile by adding (and absorbing) the nutrients necessary for each rotated crop's healthy growth.

The plants leave essential nutrients in the soil, although most farmers also add chemical fertilizer and animal manure to supply the desired levels of nutrients the crop requires. Earthworms excrete organic fertilizer, which is a valuable source of nutrients.

Like farmland and the plant life it supports, every living organism needs essential nutrients for growth, productivity, sustainability, and survival. Nutrients maintain the health of the organism's cells and provide the energy necessary for them to grow, function, and live a productive life. The smallest microorganisms (bacteria, algae, amoeba), every genus of plant life, and animals of all sizes and species, including humans, all need nutrients to live, grow, and survive.

Not all organisms require the same nutrients, amount of nutrients, or mixture of nutrients. Unrelated organisms use completely different nutrients. The main nutrients needed by plants to grow are nitrogen, phosphorus, and potassium. Within the animal kingdom, reptiles, amphibians, and mammals all require proteins, fats, carbohydrates, vitamins, minerals, and water, although the content, proportions, and eating habits all vary.

For the healthy human body, nutritional science gets updated continually on the daily requirements, percentages, ratios, and acceptable dietary intake of each of these nutrient classes. The digested nutrients absorbed into the bloodstream through capillaries that line the small intestine include water, proteins, carbohydrates, glucose, amino acids, vitamins, minerals, and fatty acids.[1] These essential elements combine with the oxygenated blood to enrich the organs and cells throughout the body.

THE NUTRIENTS IN THE BODY OF CHRIST

What does this discussion of all these organisms and the nutrients they require for growth, productivity, sustainability, and survival have to do with the Body of Christ? To answer this question, I return to the wisdom of Bishop Fulton Sheen, who explained:

> There is a hidden, mysterious, non-human, divine unifying power at work which is Charity [love] poured in the souls of the Mystical Body by the Third Person of the Blessed Trinity. A moral body [a club, a civic group] is an organization, but the Church is an organism because of its Soul.[2]

With Jesus the head, the Holy Spirit the heart and soul, and baptized Christians worldwide members of the Body, all remaining connected to Jesus, the immortal Vine, by the unity of the Holy Spirit, the Body of Christ is a living organism that is strengthened and enriched by divine nutrients. The Church receives these nutrients from the Holy Spirit; when cultivated faithfully, conscientiously, and intentionally, they promote the holiness, growth, fruitfulness, perpetuity, and power of the entire Body.

Differing from the dietary elements required by the physical human body, the nutrients essential for the healthy, living, breathing, growing, and vibrant Body of Christ are the Gifts and Fruit of the Holy Spirit.

THE GIFTS

The gifts of the Holy Spirit[3] (Isa.11:1–2) foretold for the Messiah, the Christ, the Anointed One by the prophet Isaiah were given to Jesus. These same gifts are bestowed on all Christians by the Holy Spirit at their baptism, and they are affirmed, strengthened, and reinvigorated in their souls at their confirmation (CCCC 2006, 268). "These [gifts] are permanent dispositions which make man [Christians] docile in following the promptings of the Holy Spirit" (CCC 1830).

As it relates to the human body, these gifts are the protein that energizes the members of the Body of Christ to become aware of and lovingly responsive to the nudging and inspiration we continually receive from God through the Holy Spirit. Thomas Aquinas wrote in his *Summa Theologiae*, "Therefore the gifts of the Holy Ghost are habits whereby man is perfected to obey readily the Holy Ghost" (ST, I-II, q. 68, a. 3). The gifts include wisdom, understanding, counsel, fortitude, knowledge, piety, and fear of the Lord.

The pastor of my parish wrote:

> Be expressive with the gifts of the Holy Spirit that have been given to you, and make the power of God known to those you encounter. God truly makes a difference in our lives when we activate and cultivate our stewardship of His gifts that are in us.[4]
>
> —Vy. Rev. John B. Gabage, V.F.

The Holy Spirit imbues us with these gifts, but we each must do our part to cultivate and put these gifts to use in our heart and soul so we can express them to all those we encounter to make the power of God known.

I hope that this chapter will become a resource for you that you will come back to from time to time to review the gifts and fruit, to draw inspiration to carry them with you as you play your part in the Body of Christ, and to reflect on how you're doing.

Wisdom is the gift of having an interior awareness of God's will, desires, and divine plan in our lives and for the world. Through an intimate relationship with Jesus in the Holy Spirit, we can develop right judgment so our actions, interactions, and choices (free will) can align with God's will for our good and the good of others. Wisdom allows us to view things of the world in the proper order—all created by and for the grace of God, the creator of heaven and Earth and ruler of all creation.

> We have not received the spirit of the world but the Spirit that is from God, so that we may understand the things freely given to us by God. And we speak about them not with words taught by human wisdom, but with words taught by the Spirit, describing spiritual realities in spiritual terms.
> —1 Corinthians 2:12–13

Activate and cultivate the gift of Wisdom by meditating on the Word of God and by contemplative prayer done in stillness, silence, and solitude, listening intently for the voice of Jesus through the Holy Spirit. We grow in Wisdom through experiencing the truths of our faith and by being open to and acting on the Holy Spirit's guidance for God's will in our lives.

Understanding is the gift of enlightenment into the divine truths of our faith. This gift leads us to pattern our free will in our deeds, conduct, and charity on a richer understanding of the Word of God in the Holy Scriptures in a way that deepens our relationship with God and attracts us toward the promise of eternal life.

Activate and cultivate the gift of Understanding by studying the Holy Scriptures, following the teachings of theologians past and present, regular attendance and participation in church, reception of the sacraments, and growing in your conviction of the divine truths of our faith.

Counsel is the gift of seeking and responding to God's guidance, direction, wisdom, and advice through the Holy Spirit. Right judgment and prudence are tied in closely with this gift. It is necessary to avail oneself of God's counsel in all matters, spiritual and of this world, and then to respond according to His insight and will.

Activate and cultivate the gift of Counsel by knowing the difference between right and wrong and choosing to do what is conformed to God's will. We do this by promptly asking for the Holy Spirit's guidance before acting or reacting in every circumstance. Counsel usually meets our conscience instantly when we seek it. We strengthen our propensity toward the gift of Counsel when we humble ourselves to ask for help, advice, instruction, or guidance from our family, friends, or contemporaries.

Fortitude is the gift of courage or strength in mind, heart, and will. By the power of the Holy Spirit and the grace of God, it is the ability to remain steadfast, unwavering, fully committed, determined, and uncompromising in doing good and repudiating evil. The gift of fortitude gives us confidence and trust in God's protection and His promise of eternal life, even when danger is involved. The martyrs and the saints personified the gift of fortitude.

Activate and cultivate the gift of Fortitude by growing in our trust in God through our past experiences where He protected us and helped us through difficult situations, interactions, expectations, and fears. We can grow in courage by knowing, understanding, and obeying the commandments, not only in a literal sense but in the broadest of terms. In Matthew 5:21-22, Jesus said being angry with a brother falls under the commandment of "You shall not kill." We grow in courage when we choose good over evil and receive the love, peace, and joy of God that comes from this. We can study the lives of the saints and martyrs and gain strength from their example.

Knowledge is the gift of the Holy Spirit guiding us to view all the things of the world through the lens of faith. The knowledge we receive allows us to correctly determine if something (words, thoughts, actions, intentions) is ordered properly with our faith or contrary to it. By availing ourselves of this gift, we will likely stay on the straight and narrow path that leads to love as Jesus loves.

Activate and cultivate the gift of Knowledge by strengthening our faith. We can do this by reading the Bible daily and by talking about and sharing our faith with our family, friends, and other members of the Body of Christ. We grow in faith when we listen to other's testimony and witness. We grow in faith when we become passionate about learning more and more about our faith and seek the wisdom of religious scholars and theologians. The internet makes this ever so accessible.

Piety (reverence) is the gift that allows us to be receptive to the Holy Spirit's guidance for the proper reverence, honor, devotion, and affection for God, our Father. This gift also leads all adopted children of God to love, honor, and serve one another in a familial manner because of our common relationship with the Father.

> For those who are led by the Spirit of God are children of God. For you did not receive a spirit of slavery to fall back into fear, but you received a spirit of adoption, through which we cry, "Abba, Father!" The Spirit itself bears witness with our spirit that we are children of God.
> —Romans 8:15–16

Activate and cultivate the gift of Piety (Reverence) by maturing in and expanding our worship of God, not only by attending church but by taking the love of God that is deep in our souls into our communities and sharing it with our adopted brothers and sisters, particularly those in need, beyond the physical walls of the church. We grow in Piety when we serve and honor God out of our deep love for Him, and we conduct ourselves in a way that is pleasing to Him. We can get to know God as our Father through the words of Jesus.

Fear of the Lord (awe) is the gift of being devoted to and revering God so much that we fear doing anything that would separate us from Him or cause us to lose His love. It is not fear of His just punishment for wrongdoing. Instead, it is a response we should have from the prompting of the

Holy Spirit to avoid sin out of our utmost love for God and our fear of offending Him and hurting our relationship with Him.

Activate and cultivate the gift of Fear of the Lord (Awe) by growing in our love of God. We do this by increasing our depth and regularity of prayer, examining our conscience to identify, confess, and amend moral weaknesses, listening intently for the Holy Spirit's guidance, and reading the Holy Scriptures regularly. We do this by having heartfelt gratitude for God's abundant blessings, most specifically, for the saving graces of Jesus in His passion, crucifixion, and resurrection.

We do this when we grow in humility. In *The Purpose Driven Life*, Rick Warren wrote, "Humility is not thinking less of yourself; it is thinking of yourself less."[5] Humility is thinking of yourself less while revering and loving God more. We increase in humility when we decrease in pride. Recall what John the Baptist said in his final witness after the baptism of Jesus, "He must increase; I must decrease" (John 3:30).

> I am who I am in the eyes of God—nothing more, nothing less.
> —St. Francis of Assisi

THE FRUIT

In Chapter 5's discussion of Jesus' allegory of the vine and branches, we learned that bearing fruit is essential for remaining attached to Jesus (the Vine) and living out our destiny while on Earth. One way we bear fruit is by sharing our God-given gifts and talents with others to build up the

Body of Christ, keep Jesus alive in the world, and glorify God. There is more to it, though.

In chapter 5 of his Letter to the Galatians, Paul tells us we have the freedom to act as we wish but warns, "do not use this freedom as an opportunity for the flesh, rather, serve one another through love" (v. 13). When we serve one another through love, we bear abundant fruit. The apostle says, "live by the Spirit and you will certainly not gratify the desire for the flesh. For the flesh has desires against the Spirit, and the Spirit against the flesh; these are opposed to each other, so that you may not do what you want" (vv.16–17). He then lists numerous sins of the flesh (vv. 19–21) and follows with a list of what He calls the fruit of the *Spirit* (vv. 22-23): love (charity), joy, peace, patience, kindness, generosity, faithfulness, gentleness, and self-control.[6]

The fruit are noticeable behaviors that slowly grow and mature in people who are open for the Holy Spirit to be productive in them. When we exercise the gifts of the Holy Spirit (by being more responsive to Him), these fruit become more and more evident in us. When we bear the fruit in all we are, think, and do, these essential nutrients absorb throughout the Body of Christ for serving one another through love.

What follows is a brief discussion of the fruit, using verses and quotes to help explain them and to stimulate thought on why these fruits are important in the Church. The fruits are the character traits and qualities of Jesus Christ in the Holy Spirit given to us by His presence in our hearts and souls. Some may be more evident in us than others. When we cooperate with His will for us to embody them, the fruit will naturally emanate from us in every interaction we have and in everything we do. In this way, God-the Holy Spirit-is acting through us to manifest the spiritual fruit in the Body of Christ here on Earth.

The fruit of the Spirit is the universal, all-embracing consequence of the Spirit's presence in us. All people who live in the Spirit should manifest these qualities.... When discerning whether the Spirit is living in you, in determining whether you are walking the right path, these are wonderful criteria.[7]

—Bishop Robert Barron

Charity (Love)–Infused in us by the Holy Spirit, "Charity is the theological virtue by which we love God above all things for his own sake, and our neighbor as ourselves for the love of God" (CCC 1822). God loves us unconditionally, and we are to share His unconditional love with others. This love is not a feeling; it is to will the good of the other (Aquinas) for their sake without expecting anything in return. This love is inconveniencing and sacrificial. When we love like this, we drop what we are doing and seek what is in the best interest of another person right now. This love sacrifices our time, our comfort, our ego, our money, our energy, and our desires for the good of another person. It is a forgiving love, a patient love, a consoling love, a kind love, a gentle love, a generous love, an unselfish love, and a suffering love, not only for our family, friends, and neighbors, for strangers, beggars, and even our enemies. By loving in this way, we share God's love, and love Him in return.

The love of God has been poured out into our hearts through the holy Spirit who has been given to us.

—Romans 5:5

Real love is a leaping outside of the narrow confines of my needs and desires, and an embrace of the other's good for the other's sake. It is an escape from the black hole of the ego.[8]

—Bishop Robert Barron

> What does love look like? It has the hands to help others. It has the feet to hasten to the poor and needy. It has eyes to see misery and want. It has the ears to hear the sighs and sorrows of men. That is what love looks like.
> —St. Augustine

Joy–True Christian joy comes not from things of this world but from an intimate, love relationship with God through following Jesus Christ. Joy comes from our hope in the eternal inheritance secured for us by Jesus. Joy comes in us from the love of God present in the Holy Spirit and faith and divine truth. Christian joy is one of the fruits of charity (CCC 1829). This joy is divine, most expressive when we are in God's good graces and enveloped in His love. When this joy awakens, it cannot be concealed. We exude it, and it attracts those around us.

> For today, smile and be a joyful Christian—knowing the hope that lies before you in Jesus Christ. Live out God's love, and aim to spread that joy and happiness to everyone you meet.[9]
> —Pope Francis

Peace–"A deep, abiding inner peace that comes from union with and confidence in God."[9] The peace of God comes from living and resting in his presence in the present moment undisturbed by worries about past moments or concerns for future moments. This peace gives a sense of calm and tranquility that comes from trusting God and abiding in His love even while the messy events of the fallen world persist. This peace comes from our hope for the second coming of Jesus, the Prince of Peace (Isa. 9:5), and for eternal life. This peace comes through prayer. Peace is also one of the fruits of charity (CCC 1829).

And let the peace of Christ control your hearts, the peace into which you were also called in one body. And be thankful.

—Colossians 3:15

Peace I leave with you; my peace I give to you. Not as the world gives do I give it to you. Do not let your hearts be troubled or afraid.

—John 14:27

The Lord is near. Have no anxiety at all, but in everything, by prayer and petition, with thanksgiving, make your requests known to God. Then the peace of God that surpasses all understanding will guard your hearts and minds in Christ Jesus.

—Philippians 4:6–7

Peace is a gift of God which today too must find hearts willing to receive it.[10]

—Pope Francis

Patience–This fruit is a good disposition of the mind in times of emotional difficulty, trying times, provocation, or threats of ill-will or other evil. Restraint, composure, even temper, and perseverance are all by-products of this patience when displayed with calm, mercy, understanding, and without complaining, all by the grace of God. Long-suffering is associated with this fruit when one resists being troubled when things that are good, honorable, healthy, and pure are delayed. With patience comes a willingness to acknowledge the slow person walking in front of you not only has as much of a right to be there as you but is Jesus in disguise.

Be filled with the knowledge of his will through all spiritual wisdom and understanding to live in a manner worthy of the Lord, so as to be fully pleasing, in every good work bearing fruit and growing in the knowledge of God, strengthened with every power, in accord with his glorious might, for all endurance and patience, with joy giving thanks to the Father, who has made you fit to share in the inheritance of the holy ones in light.
—Colossians 1:9–12

Then Jesus said to his disciples, "Whoever wishes to come after me must deny [humble] himself, take up his cross [his burdens patiently], and follow me."
—Matthew 16:24

Kindness–From the goodness in each of us comes the act of kindness. Kindness is goodness in action. It is not only kind words, but it also moves us to lift someone's spirits, to help satisfy their needs, to console a person who is upset or grieving, and to be encouraging. Kindness is compassionate, considerate, selfless, hospitable, helpful, thoughtful, and sometimes even anonymous.

Put on then, as God's chosen ones, holy and beloved, heartfelt compassion, kindness, humility, gentleness, and patience, bearing with one another and forgiving one another, if one has a grievance against another; as the Lord has forgiven you, so must you also do.
—Colossians 3:12–13

Giving "should be for the benefit of the recipient and not for the pleasure of it" (Van Zeller 1998).

Generosity–By His charity, Jesus' generosity was on display throughout His humanity through healing, feeding, multiplying, teaching, serving, forgiving, and ultimately dying on the cross to redeem all of humanity. In John 15:13, Jesus said, "No one has greater love than this, to lay down one's life for one's friends." While we will not be laying down our life for anyone, at least that we know of, we are to emulate the loving generosity of Jesus in our lives.

This will not be accomplished by giving out of our excesses. No, this generosity requires sacrifice and unselfish giving, not to friends and family who may be comfortable in their means and possessions, but to those family, friends, and strangers who are less fortunate, in need or experiencing hardship. This generosity involves generous giving of our prayers, love, time, treasure, hospitality, assistance, compassion, encouragement, and gifts without expectation of repayment—all for the glory of God in the name of Jesus Christ.

> For you know the gracious act of our Lord Jesus Christ, that for your sake he became poor although he was rich, so that by his poverty you might become rich.
> —2 Corinthians 8:9

> When he [Jesus] looked up he saw some wealthy people putting their offerings into the treasury and he noticed a poor widow putting in two small coins. He said, "I tell you truly, this poor widow put in more than all the rest; for those others have all made offerings from their surplus wealth, but she, from her poverty, has offered her whole livelihood."
> —Luke 21:1–4

> Never measure your generosity by what you give, but rather by what you have left.[12]
>
> —Fulton J. Sheen

Gentleness (meekness)–This fruit helps the faithful remain calm and composed when faced with a difficult situation or wrongdoing inflicted by another person. This is not "an indication of weakness but of power and strength under control. The person who possesses this quality pardons injury, corrects faults, and rules his own spirit well."[13] With this fruit, we are slow to anger, we bear offenses, personal injury, and insults patiently, and we are stern yet understanding and forgiving in correcting injustice.

> A mild answer turns back wrath, but a harsh word stirs up anger.
>
> —Proverbs 15:1

> Nothing is so strong as gentleness, nothing so gentle as real strength.
>
> —St. Francis de Sales

Faithfulness–In the first words of our Profession of Faith (Nicene Creed), we confirm, "We believe in one God, the Father, the Almighty, maker of heaven and earth, of all that is seen and unseen." Scripture explains, "Now faith is the assurance of things hoped for, the conviction of things not seen" (Heb. 11:1 RSV-CE). It occurs in the mind, heart, and soul: "By faith, man completely submits his intellect and his will to God. With his whole being man gives his assent to God the revealer" (CCC 143).

Faithfulness brings a commitment to all that God has revealed, a conviction in these divine truths passed down in the Church through the ages, and a resolve to live in accordance with God's will as taught through the Incarnate Word, Jesus, in unity with the Holy Spirit who gifts this fruit to each of us. In things of the world, faithfulness manifests in fidelity, loyalty, commitment, trustworthiness, and dedication to a spouse, loved one, or friend.

> The fruit of faith should be evident in our lives, for being a Christian is more than making sound professions of faith. It should reveal itself in practical and visible ways.
> —St. Ignatius of Antioch

Self-Control (self-mastery)–Restraint in the passions, desires, and impulses of the flesh by relying on the strength of the Holy Spirit to keep them in accordance with God's will. Only by living in the Holy Spirit can we resist and overcome temptations. The virtue of temperance and moderation in our behavior will develop self-control. With self-control, it is essential to resist both excesses and deficiencies.

> For God did not give us a spirit of cowardice but rather of power and love and self-control.
> —2 Timothy 1:7

> With all our strength and with all our effort we must strive by humility to acquire for ourselves the good gift of sober-mindedness, which can preserve us unharmed by excess from both sides. For, as the Fathers say, the extremes from both sides are equally harmful—both excess of fasting and filling the belly, excess of vigil and excessive sleep, and other excesses.
> —St. John Cassian

> The more a soul is pleasing to God, the more it must be tried.[14]
>
> —St. Pio of Pietrelcina

Let's do a quick review of the gifts and the fruit of the Holy Spirit. Our souls receive the gifts from the Holy Spirit at baptism as permanent dispositions that lead us to follow the promptings of the Spirit. The gifts are perfected in us at confirmation.

The fruit of the Holy Spirit are virtues, healthy habits, and good deeds that sprout from the gifts of the Holy Spirit who takes root in us when the soil of our soul is receptive. When we are open to God's will, we grow in holiness, and the fruit becomes more evident. The fruit slowly grows and matures in people by the grace of the Holy Spirit who provides the living water, the light, and the air that enables them to ripen with age.

How important is it for Christians to respond to the Holy Spirit by bearing plentiful fruit? Jesus shared the parable of the barren fig tree with His disciples and with us to let us know that a tree (and the People of God) must bear fruit regularly.

> There once was a person who had a fig tree planted in his orchard, and when he came in search of fruit on it but found none, he said to the gardener, "For three years now I have come in search of fruit on this fig tree but have found none. [So] cut it down (word added in the original). Why should it exhaust the soil?" He said to him in reply, "Sir, leave it for this year also, and I shall cultivate the ground around it and fertilize it; it may bear fruit in the future. If not you can cut it down."
>
> —Luke 13:6–9

What do we learn from this parable? "Jesus teaches two things—the need to produce good fruit, and the patience and tender care God spends in helping us to be good" (University of Navarre, The Navarre Bible 2001, 191). Only if we turn away from God and whither in our responsibility to bear good fruit will our tree be cut down and our branches separate from the vine. "By the power of the Spirit, God's children can bear much fruit. He who has grafted us onto the true vine will make us bear 'the fruit of the Spirit:'" (CCC 736; Gal. 5:22). There is some urgency, however. Do not delay!

Enriched with these spiritual nutrients and with Jesus and the power of the Holy Spirit within and fully around us, the Body of Christ is fortified to bear splendid fruit! However bountiful, these nutrients cannot remain hidden or suppressed inside individual Christians. We should endeavor to fertilize each other by making this fruit available for everyone we encounter, particularly those most in need. In turn, we need to be available to receive these generously from others, allowing them also to play their part in the Body of Christ. In doing so, these nutrients are transported by each blood cell (you and me) through the capillaries (as channels and vessels) to the extremities of the body and to every corner of the world.

> Christianity then is social. Isolation and individualism is its enemy, fellowship is its strength.[15]
> —Fulton J. Sheen

As we proceed through our journey of cultivating our role in the Body of Christ, we will look at practical examples of putting these principles into practice in life. The next chapter will discuss the daily sustenance needed to feed and nourish the world's strongest and largest Body.

9
NOURISHMENT

Because the Holy Spirit is the anointing of Christ, it is Christ who, as head of the Body, pours out the Spirit among his members to nourish, heal, and organize them in their mutual functions, to give them life, send them to bear witness, . . .
—CCC 739

The Spirit of humility is sweeter than honey, and those who nourish themselves with this honey produce sweet fruit.
—St. Anthony of Padua

Prayer is a pasturage, a field, wherein all the virtues find their nourishment, growth, and strength.
—St. Catherine of Siena

I will willingly abandon this miserable body to hunger and suffering, provided that my soul may have its ordinary nourishment.
—St. Kateri Tekakwitha

Many saints over the centuries have referred to the sacraments, virtues, and other spiritual practices—Scripture reading, repentance, prayer—as nourishment for the soul. Undoubtedly, there is no better way to nourish the soul than by living a Christ-centered and virtuous life. When this is multiplied throughout the Body of Christ, the benefits to Christianity and to the world are enormous.

There were two instances in the Bible where Jesus performed the miracle of the multiplication—both involving a few loaves of bread and some fish multiplied to feed thousands of people who had traveled to see and listen to Him and to bring loved ones for His healing.[1] The notes on Mark 6:30–44 (University of Navarre, The Navarre Bible 2001, 105–106) explain the miracle in this way:

> In the miracle of the loaves Jesus' attitude sets an example for the Christian. When he sees the state of the people, he is filled with compassion and he gives them nourishment for both soul and body—the spiritual nourishment of his teaching, and the bread as bodily food. . . . The scene is also a figure to the new People of God, which gets its nourishment from the word of Christ and the bread of the Eucharist.

The three people quoted at the beginning of this chapter, and thousands of others, made frequent consumption of this spiritual nourishment a top priority, and they fulfilled their saintly calling.

Spiritual nourishment is essential for the sanctity of our souls, for we are all called to be holy and to live as saints. The more we consume, the more open and attentive we will be to living in accordance with the will of God moment by moment. Being open to God's will every moment is the definition of living a holy life.

As we seek to play our part in the Body of Christ and what we do is aligned with God's will, He just might multiply our efforts, He just might magnify our gifts and talents, and He could very well use us to nourish the crowds. This would be accomplished through the presence and guidance of the Holy Spirit and the spiritual and physical actions we take to do our part to nourish this Body. The more spiritual nourishment we consume individually, the more inclined we will be to take nourishing action in our communities and in the Body of Christ throughout the world.

Think about everything St. Teresa of Calcutta (Mother Teresa) accomplished in and around Calcutta and for the world. She was a profoundly devout nun who prayed fervently. She left the comforts of a convent to live in the slums to help the "poorest of the poor." With no funding and relying on the grace of God by begging and praying for donations and volunteers, she began her missionary work in 1948. She founded a new religious order in 1950, the Missionaries of Charities. At the time of her death in 1997, more than 4000 sisters had joined her order and were carrying out her mission in over 100 countries.

Did God multiply Mother Teresa's efforts and use her to nourish the poorest of the poor? In her words:

> On my first trip along the streets of Calcutta, a priest came up to me. He asked me to give a contribution to a collection for the Catholic press. I had left with five rupees, and I had already given four of them to the poor. I hesitated, then gave the priest the one that

remained. That afternoon, the same priest came to see me and brought an envelope. He told me that a man had given him the envelope because he had heard about my projects and wanted to help me. There were fifty rupees in that envelope. I had the feeling, at that moment, that God had begun to bless the work and would never abandon me.

THE KINGDOM OF GOD . . .

In a word, the kingdom of God is the manifestation and the realization of God's plan of salvation in all its fullness.
—St. John Paul II (*Redemptoris Missio,* 1990, II, 15)

When Jesus began His ministry in Galilee, He proclaimed, "The kingdom of God is at hand: repent, and believe in the gospel" (Mark 1:15). The kingdom that the Son of God was declaring was present in Himself, the Christ, the Messiah. "This kingdom shone out before men in the word, in the works, and in the presence of Christ"[2] (*Lumen Gentium* # 5; CCC 567).

Jesus preached about the kingdom of God and extended an invitation to everyone to enter it using parables—short earthly stories that had a spiritual meaning. Seven such parables were recorded in the 13th chapter of Matthew's Gospel. To enter the kingdom, a person must "repent and believe in the gospel." Many of the Jewish faith chose not to believe. Jesus used these parables to teach but also to conceal the true meaning of the kingdom of God to the nonbelievers of His time whose hearts were closed to the Messiah. In Mark 4:11–12 (RSV-CE), Jesus said, "To you has been given the secret of the kingdom of God, but for those outside everything is in parables; so that they may indeed see but not perceive and may indeed hear but not understand; *lest they should turn again and be forgiven*" (emphasis added). In Matthew 13:10–11 (RSV-CE), the evangelist wrote, "Then the disciples came and said to him, 'Why do you speak to them in parables?' And he answered them, 'To you it has been given to know the secrets of the kingdom of heaven, but to them it has not been given.'"

Referencing these verses, the *Catechism* states, "Jesus and the presence of the kingdom in this world are secretly at the heart of the parables. One must enter the kingdom, that is, become a disciple of Christ, to 'know the secrets of the kingdom of heaven.' For those who stay 'outside,' everything remains enigmatic" (CCC 546).

Jesus unveiled the secret meaning of the parables to the disciples, and He continues to do this for those of us who follow Him and His teachings today. "All are invited by Jesus to enter the Kingdom of God. Even the worst of sinners is called to convert and to accept the boundless mercy of the Father. Already here on earth, the Kingdom belongs to those who accept it with a humble heart. To them the mysteries of the Kingdom are revealed" (CCCC 2006, 107).

. . . Is At Hand

When we pray the Lord's Prayer, we petition the Father, "thy kingdom come." What we are asking of God is twofold. "The Church prays for the final coming of the Kingdom of God through Christ's return in glory. The Church prays also that the Kingdom of God increase from now on through people's sanctification in the Spirit and through their commitment to the service of justice and peace" (CCCC 2006, 590).

The kingdom of God here and now is with us in the Church, the Body of Christ. The Pastor of my parish, Vy. Rev. John B Gabage, V.F., often reminds the congregation that the kingdom of God is at hand—at your hand, at my hand, at our hands. As disciples of Jesus Christ, it is our responsibility to extend our hands to share the love of God in visible and concrete ways so we can remain committed to doing our part to increase the kingdom through our sanctification in the Holy Spirit. It is through the spiritual and visible action we take that the soul of the Church, the Holy Spirit, nourishes the Body of Christ.

Nourishment gives the human body energy, supports muscle contraction, boosts metabolism, and helps the Body of Christ function. It builds trust, encourages cooperation, enhances vision, breeds boldness, calms fear, fosters interaction, spreads peace, and keeps Jesus alive in the world.

> Christ has no body now, but yours. No hands, no feet on earth, but yours.
> —St. Teresa of Avila

Perhaps the most well-known of the parables is that which compares the kingdom of God to the mustard seed (Matt. 13:31–32). "It is the smallest of all the seeds, yet when full-grown it is the largest of plants" (v. 32). God plants tiny seeds of purpose in each of us that He wants us to cultivate in our own God-given style in cooperation with the Holy Spirit.

As these seeds sprout and grow in and through us, they can take root, build a sturdy foundation, and spread according to God's plan. Some may become small yet fruitful plants in your backyard or your community. Others may grow like the mustard seed, branching out in all directions and touching multitudes by the grace of God. The point is this: we need to be aware of the invitation to act when God plants that seedling, and we must respond in the affirmative so that God's kingdom will grow through us.

Nowhere is this more formative than in our own families. God gives us seeds to plant in our children through love, faith, prayer, encouragement, praise, discipline, forgiveness, humility, opportunity, kindness, and protection. As these and other seeds grow in them, our children will mature into the next generation of the kingdom of God on Earth—invited into action to cultivate the seeds they receive from the Father.

As parents, grandparents, aunts, uncles, and brothers and sisters, the example we give to our younger family members is imitated and, over time, tends to become an ingrained trait or habit in them. Therefore, it is crucial to exemplify faithfulness, Christ-centeredness, prayerfulness, love of neighbor, humility, and a giving spirit—all nourishing elements for them and the Body of Christ. If we do this well, our children will want to participate with us in acts of charity and service at an early age, and they will carry this passion through adolescence, early adulthood, and life.

As Christians and disciples of Jesus, we are "created in Christ Jesus" to perform acts of charity or "the good works that God has prepared in advance" (Eph. 2:10). Jesus spoke explicitly about what He expects of us. I will touch on a few of those actions: trust Him, love the poor, be His witnesses, and give of yourself.

TRUST AND ACT

There are many opportunities around us every day to help those in need. So often, though, we pull back from doing anything because the situation may make us uncomfortable. Think about the vehicle stopped on the side of the highway. As we approach it at speed, many thoughts may cross our minds. I'm going too fast to stop now. I need to get to work. That vehicle looks shady. I don't know those people. There are three of them and one of me. What might they do to me if I stop? There are too many crazy people out there; I shouldn't put myself in danger. Maybe they have already called for help.

This scenario is a modern-day version of the parable of the Good Samaritan (Luke 10: 29–37). In response to the question "And who is my neighbor?" (v. 29), Jesus tells the story of a man who was robbed, stripped, beaten, and left to die on the side of the road. A priest and then a Levite (an official who served in the Temple) came upon the victim but passed on the opposite side of this dangerous road. A Samaritan traveler who came up to him was "moved with compassion at the sight" (v. 33). He bandaged the man, put him on his own animal, and took him to an inn to care for him (v. 34). The Samaritan then gave the innkeeper some money and asked him to take care of the man until the traveler returned to settle his debts.

Because of their centuries-old paganistic approach to Judaism, the Samaritans were outcasts who were looked down upon with hatred by the Jews. In showing the lack of compassion of the priest and the Levite in contrast to the goodness of the Samaritan, Jesus again showed His compassion and mercy for the outcast and sinners, and He wants us to do the same.

Jesus asked the law scholar who posed the question of which of the three passersby was a neighbor to the victim. The scholar answered, "The one who treated him with mercy." Jesus said, "Go and do likewise" (v. 37).

To be sure, Jesus wouldn't want us to place ourselves in a situation of apparent danger. In such an instance, we could still make a phone call to send help to the people stranded on the highway and even say a prayer for their safety. If this situation occurred in broad daylight on a well-traveled thoroughfare, Jesus would probably expect us to do more.

The victim in this parable can also represent a friend beaten, robbed, and stripped by sin. Jesus wants us to help them, not by judging them, but with humility and understanding as we seek to help them get back on the righteous path.

We need to place our trust in the Lord. Throughout the Bible, we are encouraged to trust the Lord and repeatedly told to "be not afraid." Trust in God nourishes the soul and provides essential nourishment for taking action in the Body of Christ.

> Do not let your hearts be troubled. You have faith in God; have faith also in me.
> —John 14:1

> I command you: be strong and steadfast! Do not fear nor be dismayed, for the LORD, your God, is with you wherever you go.
> —Joshua 1:9

> Blessed are those who trust in the LORD; the LORD will be their trust. They are like a tree planted beside the waters that stretches out its roots to the stream: It does not fear heat when it comes, its leaves stay green; In the

year of drought it shows no distress, but still produces fruit.

—Jeremiah 17:7-8

God is with us wherever we go. When Moses was afraid upon hearing God had commissioned him to lead the Israelites out of Egypt, the Lord told him, "I will be with you" (Exod. 3:12). He not only desires for us to bear good fruit, but He is right there with us and cheering us on.

In those times when our initial reaction is to resist, or to be afraid, take a deep breath. Ask God what He would like you to do. Say a quick prayer, "Jesus, I trust in you." Then reassess the situation to see if peace has come over you. If so, be willing to step outside your comfort zone. Trust and take that action God has placed in front of you to "Go and do likewise" and to be "The one who treated him with mercy."

LOVE THE LEAST

In His humanity, Jesus Christ associated with the poor, the deprived, the underprivileged, those at the fringes of society, the sick, and the spiritually impoverished. Collectively, all who experience these conditions are considered poor and are worthy of our love and works of charity and justice. Not only are they worthy of our love, but Jesus also commanded that we provide for them. He commanded that we love and provide for them and warned if we withhold from doing any of this, we are turning our backs on Jesus Himself, the Son of God.

One of the best-known teachings of Jesus is in the Gospel of Matthew (25:31–46). Christ was describing the

Last Judgment upon His second coming, and He gave a detailed list of what He expects from us:

- Feed the hungry.
- Give drink to the thirsty.
- Welcome the stranger.
- Clothe the naked.
- Care for the sick.
- Visit the imprisoned.

To those who take this action, Jesus said, "Amen, I say to you, whatever you did for one of these least brothers of mine, you did for me" (v. 40). Those who decline to love the least of their brothers and sisters in this way turn their backs on Jesus, for He said, "what you did not do for one of these least ones, you did not do for me" (v. 45). Jesus then issued this stark warning: "And these will go off to eternal punishment, but the righteous to eternal life" (v. 46).

Just like when Jesus was mistaken as the gardener by Mary Magdalene outside the tomb on the first Easter and soon after when He shielded His resurrected identity from the two disciples on the road to Emmaus, you and I should expect that everyone we encounter in our lives is also Jesus in disguise. These examples should encourage us to love our neighbor and to be aware of the opportunities presented to us to do acts of charity.

> If you want to find God, seek him where he is hidden: in the neediest, the sick, the hungry, the imprisoned.[3]
> —Pope Francis

Although there are differences between Christians on the merits of good works in our salvation, I believe most would agree that loving our neighbor necessitates doing acts of love in some form or fashion. It is human nature because God has inscribed love on our hearts. As St. Thérèse of Lisieux said, "Let us love, for that is what our hearts were made for." Try not to get hung up on whether people refer to them as works of mercy, acts of service, acts of charity, works of piety, good works, or works. The importance of all of this is to love God and to love our neighbor.

In addition to the list that Jesus gave us in Matthew 25, there are more actions we can and should take to nourish and build up the Body of Christ. Some of them include sheltering the homeless, consoling the grieving and burying the dead, offering hospitality, instructing, counseling, and advising those who are doubtful or do not believe in our faith, forgiving and bearing wrongs patiently, encouraging others, praying for the living and the dead, and generous giving of financial resources and material goods to those in need.

> If someone who has worldly means sees a brother in need and refuses him compassion, how can the love of God remain in him? Children, let us love not in word or speech but in deed and truth.
> —1 John 3:16–18

> If you lavish your food on the hungry and satisfy the afflicted; Then your light shall rise in the darkness, and your gloom shall become like midday.
> —Isaiah 58:10

> Good works are links that form a chain of love.
> —St. Teresa of Calcutta

This chain of love links the members of the Body of Christ with each other and those in need.

BE HIS WITNESSES

Evangelization—it's not a bad word. Candidly, I would cringe at the thought of evangelizing before I had a chance to understand what it means and the many forms it can take. To be sure, in the strictest sense, to evangelize is to share the Good News of the Gospel, that is, to proclaim that Jesus died on the cross and rose from the dead to save the world from sin and evil and to bless us with eternal life in heaven.

The Greek word *evangelion* means "good news" or "good tidings." Jesus is the Good News who came to "bring glad tidings to the poor" (Luke 4:18). As the Incarnate Word of God made flesh, He was evangelist par excellence. Not only did Jesus spread the Good News recorded in the Gospels, but He also lived the Good News of the Gospel. His life was and is the Good News. His life spoke and exhibited the Word right down to His passion, death on the cross, resurrection, and ascension into heaven.

As we can see from Jesus' example, evangelization has many forms. It is not only through sharing (speaking) the Good News that one evangelizes, but also by "radiating the love of Jesus by the everyday way we speak, think, and act"[4] that we exemplify the good tidings Jesus brought into the world. When we live our faith daily, we strengthen our relationship with Jesus, and we become His witnesses in the world. The goal of evangelization is to reach nonbelievers in a way that inspires them to contemplate the Good News so the Holy Spirit can fill their hearts with faith, hope, and love and lead them to baptism. We can also evangelize in the Body of Christ by helping believers. All of us, as believers, still falter, which is why I get comfort from sharing faith and discussion with fellow believers.

> But you will receive power when the holy Spirit comes upon you, and you will be my witnesses in Jerusalem, throughout Judea and Samaria, and to the ends of the earth.
> —Acts 1:8

Evangelization does not happen in any form were it not by the power of the Holy Spirit. The Holy Spirit is the soul of the Body of Christ and resides in the soul of every member. Evangelization starts in and with the Church and with every Christian. As Bishop Barron wrote, "The Church is an announcing, proclaiming, and evangelizing organism."[5] St. Paul told the early church in Corinth, "So we are ambassadors for Christ, as if God were appealing through us" (2 Cor. 5:20).

Take on roles in your church. Be a lector or reader, become an usher, collect the offering, join the choir, be an acolyte, alter server, or greeter, be a Eucharistic minister, join or lead the youth group, become a catechist or Sunday school teacher, a traffic director, a tutor, or just be available to help the Pastor in any way you can. The example you set will inspire others to do their part and positively influence the faith formation of the younger members.

Your faith witness outside of the church is just as important as it is in the church. As members of Christian congregations around the world, it is both the pastoral responsibility and that of the laity to carry Christ beyond the pews, beyond the walls of the building, into the community. We carry the love of Christ in our hearts, and we are called as witnesses to share His love everywhere we go, and in all that we do and speak. We need to spread the Gospel in word and by exemplifying how Jesus lived during His three-year ministry. Do what the Holy Spirit places on your heart and what is most comfortable for you intending to live your faith and spread the Good News in the name of Jesus Christ.

Community outreach ministries are a great example of evangelization in action. Homeless shelters, food pantries, days of free access to dental and medical care, backpack programs for children in schools, free tutoring, community clean-up opportunities, donations of food, time, clothing, necessities, and money, prayer groups, groups that support the church and philanthropy, and the many volunteers who staff all these ministries all bear witness to the Gospel and the life of Christ.

We witness when we speak, teach, mentor, remind, share, and testify on the Good News. We witness when we get involved in the abundant organized outreach ministries in our communities and on a larger scale. We witness by the missionary work that many perform in desolate and impoverished regions around the world.

The witnessing action we take can be as organized and deliberate as described above. Critically though, it also extends from us by living our faith relationship with God every day, minute by minute. We witness by our service, we witness by our humility, we witness by our joy, by our gait, our smile, our love, our justice, our compassion, our faithfulness, our peace, our suffering, our prayer, our relationships, our family, our patience, our concern, our support, our sympathy, our encouragement, our generosity, our poverty, our obedience, our charity, our help, and by sharing burdens. We witness by our witness.

To witness well, our actions must be Christ-like and consistent with the teachings of the Gospels and the verbal witness we share. Jesus said of the scribes and Pharisees, "For they preach but they do not practice" (Matt. 23:3). We must practice what we preach, walk the talk, and do what we say.

Actions speak louder than words; let your words teach and your actions speak.
—St. Anthony of Padua

In God's eyes, words have only the value of our actions.
—St. Ignatius of Loyola

We are witnesses of these things, as is the holy Spirit that God has given to those who obey him.
—Acts 5:32

GIVE GENEROUSLY

Giving alms is an act of charity using financial or material means to help those in need. It is donating money, goods, or services to those who are less fortunate, and it is "also a work of justice pleasing to God" (CCC 2462) instructed in the Old and New Testaments.

> Give alms from your possessions. Do not turn your face away from any of the poor, so that God's face will not be turned away from you. Give in proportion to what you own. If you have great wealth, give alms out of your abundance; if you have but little, do not be afraid to give alms even of that little. You will be storing up a goodly treasure for yourself against the day of adversity.
> —Tobit 4:7–9

When you give, give generously and not with a stingy heart; for that, the LORD, your God, will bless you in all your works and undertakings. The land will never lack for needy persons; that is why I command you:

"Open your hand freely to your poor and to your needy kin in your land."
—Deuteronomy 15:10–11

But as to what is within, give alms, and behold, everything will be clean for you.
—Luke 11:41

Almsgiving is widely observed throughout Christianity. Some may give through a financial offering in the weekly Sunday collection, donations made to charitable organizations, or directly to those in need encountered on the street and in our communities. Some Christians may do all of these. Others may donate their time volunteering. Many piggy banks gets raided or broken too as children play their part.

The habit of giving only enhances the desire to give.
—Walt Whitman

Where almsgiving is directed is not quite as important as how it is performed. Giving with a generous heart, with some sacrifice, and without the expectation of receiving anything in return is the message here. Almsgiving can tie in with fasting in that we could give up some activities or luxuries (eating out one less time a week, for example) to make those funds available to those in need.

When we empty ourselves of these desires, we open space for God to fill with His love, and we share that love with others by giving generously. In doing this, we emulate the humbling, self-emptying, and sacrificial love of Jesus. We emulate the merciful love of Jesus for our neighbor.

The Greek origin of the word alms means mercy and compassion. Not only is almsgiving an act of charity, but it is also an act of mercy that goes along with everything noted previously in the Love the Least section. The merciful heart will see the merciful Jesus in the eyes of those in need.

This giving of self is expected without seeking recognition or reward. It should be out of our humility, not out of our egos, that we give. In Matthew 6:1–4, Jesus taught about almsgiving in the Sermon on the Mount, saying this:

> [But] take care not to perform righteous deeds in order that people may see them; otherwise, you will have no recompense from your heavenly Father. When you give alms, do not blow a trumpet before you, as the hypocrites do in the synagogues and in the streets to win the praise of others. Amen, I say to you, they have received their reward. But when you give alms, do not let your left hand know what your right is doing, so that your almsgiving may be secret. And your Father who sees in secret will repay you.

We have all probably heard someone say, "I am going to spend everything I have before I die down to my last penny. You can't take it with you!" No, you cannot take what you have received into eternal life. You may be able to bring along what you have given, though. St. Paul shared something Jesus once said that emphasizes this. "Keep in mind the words of the Lord Jesus who Himself said, 'It is more blessed to give than to receive'" (Acts 20:35). Jesus' quote, and thought-provoking remarks made by beloved saints, might change the outlook of some planning to spend everything they have.

> A sacrifice to be real must cost, must hurt, must empty ourselves.
> —St. Teresa of Calcutta

Remember that when you leave this earth, you can take with you nothing that you have received—but only what you have given; a full heart enriched by honest service, love, sacrifice, and courage.

—St. Francis of Assisi

In one of his *Formed Daily Reflections*,[6] Dr. Tim Gray, President of the Augustine Institute, tells us, "What you gave goes with you (into eternity), what you have doesn't," referencing Mark 9:41 and Psalm 49. Dr. Gray points to James 5:1–3 to say what we hoard and don't share "will be a testimony against you" (v. 3). His suggestion is to ask ourselves, "what have I given, and what do I have?" Some may realize they "have so much and have shared so little." It's never too late to start.

A healthy heart is essential for a strong, healthy, and energetic body. The heart's rhythmic pumping action must be sufficient. Otherwise, the blood cells would not fill with oxygen, water, and other nutrients or be transported throughout the body.

Members of the Body of Christ must also have a heart-healthy regimen to maintain the holiness, strength, good health, and energy needed to play their unique part, pull their weight, and fulfill their calling. The essential element for this is discussed in the next chapter.

10
A HEALTHY HEART

Blessed are those who keep his testimonies,
who seek him with all their heart.
—Psalm 119:2

When you call me, and come and pray to me, I will listen to you. When you look for me, you will find me. Yes, when you seek me with all your heart, I will let you find me...
—Jeremiah 29:12–14

According to Scripture, it is the heart that prays. If our heart is far from God, the words of prayer are in vain.
—CCC 2562

Ever wonder why the human heart is associated with love?

We are what we eat. While somewhat trite, this phrase holds a lot of truth. The healthiness of the human heart and circulatory system is related to the type and amount of food, drink, sweets, sodium, and snacks we ingest. Genetics and the amount of exercise we get are also factors. Adverse effects include smoking, heavy consumption of alcohol, and illicit drug usage.

A high-calorie diet full of saturated fats, sugars, sodium, and junk food, is a recipe for weight gain, diabetes, and heart disease. A heart-healthy diet that includes a variety of fruits and vegetables, and fiber, is low in saturated fats and limits the number of calories can improve the health of the heart, mind, and body. Combine this with regular physical activity, and a person will likely feel well and be in better shape.

In the Body of Christ, we are what we consume. This Body thrives on the spiritual communion between the Trinity and the People of God. It is healthiest when the Body works in unity with the heart and soul (the Holy Spirit) to keep Jesus (the head) alive in the world as we work together to carry out the will of God here on Earth.

It becomes necessary, then, that the individual members of the Body consume a healthy diet of spiritual sustenance that includes frequent reception of Holy Communion, regular participation in the worship, repentance of sins, reading and meditating on God's Word in the Bible, tapping resources by spiritual leaders and theologians, and fellowship and collaboration with other members of the Body of Christ. And because it is the heart that prays, this Body becomes strong when it consumes a substantial diet of prayer.

> You don't know how to pray? Put yourself in the presence of God, and as soon as you have said, "Lord, I don't know how to pray!" you can be sure you've already begun.
> —St. Josemaría Escrivá (*The Way*, 1982, 30)

If there is one main thing all humans have in common, one thing that unifies every person ever created, it is "God calls every being from nothingness into existence." (While nonbelievers might argue this central tenet, debating this is beyond the scope of these pages.) Even in sin, all humanity "retains the desire for the one who calls him into existence" (CCC 2566). *The Catechism* also states, "The desire for God is written in the human heart, because man is created by God and for God; and God never ceases to draw man to himself" (CCC 27).

In general, prayer unites the religions of the world. All Christians have this desire to be in communion with God, to receive God's love and to love Him in return, to communicate with God, to express praise and gratitude to God, to adore God, and to seek the help of God for themselves, their loved ones, and for others.

Have you ever thought about how God is so loving that He, our Creator and Ruler of all Creation, desires an intimate relationship with each one of His created children? He not only wants this relationship, but He has invited us into it and waits lovingly and patiently for us to "Draw near to God, and he will draw near to you" (James 4:8). I have heard many doubters say something along the lines of "I just don't know. I am waiting for God." The point they are missing is that He is waiting for them to make the first move toward Him. God will then be "all-in." That first move usually comes in the form of prayer.

As we discussed earlier, God always initiates prayer in us. God invites us into communion with Him, into a dialogue with Him, and into His presence through the gift of prayer.

Jesus prayed to the Father continually. There are numerous instances recorded in the Bible where Jesus prayed publicly and went off to pray in solitude (Luke 5:16). Jesus exhibits the importance of prayer. He shows us how to approach our heavenly Father in prayer. He encourages us to pray with great confidence that the Father will listen and answer our prayers if they conform to His will.

> Therefore I tell you, all that you ask for in prayer, believe that you will receive it and it shall be yours.
> —Mark 11:24

> Whatever you ask for in prayer with faith, you will receive.
> —Matthew 21:22

> Ask and it will be given to you; seek and you will find; knock and the door will be opened to you. For everyone who asks, receives; and the one who seeks, finds; and to the one who knocks, the door will be opened.
> —Matthew 7:7–8

Having been crucified, raised from the dead, and taken up into heaven, Jesus is now seated at the right hand of the Father on the throne of God. Jesus is our heavenly intercessor and mediator with God the Father (Rom. 8:34). When we pray through Jesus, He brings our prayers straight to the Father.

> Therefore, he is always able to save those who approach God through him, since he lives forever to make intercession for them.
> —Hebrews 7:25

It is the Holy Spirit who prays through us and with us. The Holy Spirit teaches the Body of Christ to pray, and prayer "extends throughout" it (CCC 2565). In most cases, we have a sense of when our prayers are properly aligned with the will of God, although we have no way of knowing with certainty if everything we bring to God in prayer conforms with His will. The Holy Spirit does, though, and He is our advocate and intercessor in prayer.

> Likewise the Spirit helps us in our weakness; for we do not know how to pray as we ought, but the Spirit himself intercedes for us with sighs too deep for words. And he who searches the hearts of men knows what is the mind of the Spirit, because the Spirit intercedes for the saints according to the will of God.
> —Romans 8:26–27 (RSV-CE)

There are several forms of Christian prayer. These forms are generally consistent across the different Churches and communities with some variation in number and expression. The primary forms of prayer include blessing and adoration, petition and intercession, and thanksgiving and praise.* Lifting our hearts and souls to God in these forms of prayer is essential for every Christian if we are to grow in faith and embrace a personal relationship with the Holy Trinity and the one true God (CCC 2558).

As we receive God's abundant blessings, bless Him in return, and give thanks for His divine providence in all that

---

* A brief explanation of these forms of prayer can be found online in the Catechism of the Catholic Church on page 636, paragraph 2644, and following.

we are, have, and experience, we praise Him, giving Him all the glory in everything. Through this attitude, our hearts and minds can join in a loving and peaceful disposition to carry out our collective mission in the Body of Christ.

For a moment, let us focus on a prayer of petition, specifically intercession, because of its importance in the Body of Christ and the part every member plays in it.

No matter how small and insignificant or large and extraordinary you feel your efforts may be, everything you do in the name of Jesus is a prayer that builds up the Body of Christ. Everything you do in this manner is an act of ministry. In one of his *Daily Gospel Reflections*, Bishop Barron said, "Prayer is not incidental to ministry. . . . It is the lifeblood of the Church's efforts. Without it, nothing will succeed."[1]

From Philippians 4:6, St. Paul writes while in prison: "Have no anxiety at all, but in everything, by prayer and petition, with thanksgiving, make your requests known to God."

Prayer of petition involves asking God, with humility and contrition, for His mercy and forgiveness. It consists in pleading for and seeking the kingdom of God. And it involves praying for everything we feel we need, particularly what we perceive to be in accord with God's will.

Intercession is a prayer of petition where we pray to God in the interest of others—family, friends, classmates, colleagues, and church members and pastors. Many other people in our lives or whom we hear or read about may also need our prayers.

Prayers of intercession should not only be local or for familiar faces. They should extend beyond our family unit and our zip code. Prayers of intercession "knows no boundaries" (CCC 2647).

St. Paul taught us to "pray without ceasing" (1 Thess. 5:17) and "at every opportunity in the Spirit. . ..for all the holy ones" (Eph. 6:18). In other words, as members of the Body of Christ, it is incumbent on us to always be looking for opportunities to offer prayers for others—intercessory prayers for healing, hope, faith, sobriety, success, good health, and so much more. Sharing each other's burdens is one of our obligations in the Body of Christ. It is paramount that we listen for the Holy Spirit's prompting and that we respond in prayer when he does.

Intercession comes naturally when family, loved ones, and close friends are involved. When word spreads that someone needs our prayers, the Holy Spirit can inspire our loving hearts and lead us there. When the need for prayer extends beyond our family and social circle our efforts tend to diminish. We may say a quick prayer upon hearing of a situation, although it often quickly slips our minds. Due to the busy pace of life, we also tend to be less attuned to opportunities for prayer when they are not right on our doorstep.

By the grace of God, many churches have prayer chains or prayer groups that leap into action when made aware of the need for prayer. These prayer warriors keep these intentions in their hearts and minds and fulfill an important role in the Body of Christ. Often, the person for whom they may be praying is a stranger known only in name and intention, though they pray on in love. Many faithful who have chosen the consecrated life are "set apart" to live a life of fervent prayer, including intercessory prayer that reaches to God for those whom they offer it.

When you call me, and come and pray to me, I will listen to you.
—Jeremiah 29:12

Allow me to suggest some everyday scenarios that lend to prayers of intercession. We can always offer prayers for groups like the homeless, the addicted, victims of natural disasters, and others in need. We can intercede for the organizations that provide services to these groups of people and those who staff them and volunteer. We can pray for others who take it upon themselves to meet these people where they are and to look them in the eyes. The opportunities for intercessory prayer of this nature are endless. Pick one or two that resonate with you and set aside a period (a week, a month, during Lent, for example) where you intercede in prayer for them; then move on to other intentions of importance for you.

Specifically, we can increase our awareness of individuals who may need our intercession. Some are obvious. The person who falls ill at church gets lifted in an abundance of prayer. Many pray for anyone in public needing emergency care. We pray for victims of car accidents we see.

Some situations where intercessory prayer would be fruitful are less obvious because they are removed from us by distance or emotional ties or are outside our line of sight.

- Perhaps you are at home, and you hear the sirens of fire equipment rushing to the aid of someone in your vicinity. Offer a prayer to prevent bodily harm and property loss and for the safety of the responders. Offer a prayer for those in this distress to feel God's presence.
- You notice a classmate seems sad and gloomy. Prayers that Jesus will help him resolve the feelings

and lift his spirits would benefit this person. A kind word or gesture you give to him could also be offered up in prayer.
- You hear in the news of a family suffering from a medical concern that has caused them financial hardship. Your prayers for healing, donations, and financial assistance would be well received when offered through Christ our Lord. A donation of your own to a charitable fund in their name could be offered in prayer.
- You notice a prison road crew on the side of the highway collecting trash. Prayers that they have or will turn their lives over to Jesus, accept a second chance to be a responsible member of society, and have access to God's spiritual works and prison chaplains would all be loving and merciful.
- You drive by a cemetery where people are gathering for the funeral of a loved one. Prayers for the departed soul and the comforting and consolation for the family can be quietly offered from your heart.
- A shopper at the grocery store is exhibiting impatience and irritation with a store clerk. Prayers for humility and peace in his heart and emotional support for the young clerk can be offered.
- Christians are being persecuted and harmed for their faith. How powerful it would be if the entire Body of Christ lifted these poor brothers and sisters in prayer.

These are examples and suggestions intended to arouse the heart and stir thought. The opportunities for prayers of petition and intercession become plentiful when we increase in awareness and when the Holy Spirit inspires our minds and hearts to live in a state of prayer.

> There are more tears shed over answered prayers than over unanswered prayers.
> —St. Teresa of Avila

I want to leave you with a few general comments on prayer, along with relevant verses and quotes.

We are encouraged to pray for each other when we step off the straight and narrow path and have fallen into sin. This also is a form of intercessory prayer noted by the apostle James:

> Therefore, confess your sins to one another and pray for one another, that you may be healed.
> —James 5:16

> He was in such agony and he prayed so fervently that his sweat became like drops of blood falling on the ground.
> —Luke 22:44

How should we pray? As Jesus did in His agony in the garden, the apostles instruct us to pray with fervor in our hearts, not to the point of sweating blood but with intensity, passionate feeling, and great emotion. A heartfelt prayer, with humility, has a better chance of being heard and answered than a prayer with arrogant and selfish intentions.

> The fervent prayer of a righteous person is very powerful.
> —James 5:16

A HEALTHY HEART

> Peter thus was being kept in prison, but prayer by the church was fervently being made to God on his behalf.
> —Acts 12:5

Whether we spend an hour in prayer or say a few quick words, any prayer needs to come from the heart with intensity, passion, and emotion. Think for a minute about all the prayer requests posted on social media. So many respond with multiple "praying hands" emojis. The higher number of these typically signifies a greater intensity of prayer. There is no doubt that the responders intend to offer heartfelt comfort to those asking for prayers. But I ponder whether those posting these emojis follow up with fervent prayer.

We learn from The Word of God, some of the Saints, and our own experiences that fervent prayer is more efficacious than prayer that lacks emotion or passion.

> Whether or not our prayer is heard depends not on the number of words, but on the fervor of our souls.
> —St. John Chrysostom

> Your Father knows what you need before you ask him.
> —Matthew 6:8

We must also pray with persistence. Try to not be discouraged when you feel your prayers are not answered. Your prayer may not align with God's will for you, or God's path for refinement may not meet your timeline. In God's wisdom, it could be the case that He knows that you are not ready to receive that for which you are asking. Keep praying through Christ, our Lord. If your desires do not conform with God's plan, He will slowly change your heart, so you "enter into the desire of the Spirit" (CCC 2737). Keep praying in the name of Jesus. As your desires align more with God's plan, your prayer will be more in line with God's plan. When our requests are in line with God's will, our prayers will be answered, albeit on God's timeline, not ours. Keep praying through Christ, our Lord.

> Then he told them a parable about the necessity for them to pray always without becoming weary.
> —Luke 18:1

> The desire of the heart is thy prayers; and if thy desire is without ceasing, thy prayer will also be without ceasing. The continuance of your longing is the continuance of your prayer.
> —St. Augustine, *Exposition on the Book of Psalms*

For our prayers to be heard, it matters not the number of words. Prayer is expected to be a dialogue, and it is pretty difficult to hear what God is saying if we aren't listening, and we cannot listen if we do all the talking.

Just before Jesus taught the apostles how to pray, he told them:

> In praying, do not babble like the pagans, who think that they will be heard because of their many words.
> —Matthew 6:7

Jesus then gave them the Lord's Prayer—a five-verse all-encompassing prayer directed to "Our Father" for

2000 years. This 52-word prayer is likely the most recited Christian prayer since the time of Jesus.

> One need not say much to pray well.
> —St. John Vianney

We can pray always and anywhere, and we should. There is a time and place to pull aside for private interior prayer or for vocal prayer that may be more structured or lengthy. There is even more time throughout our daily routines when we can say "breath prayers."

We can whisper these short prayers while we are on the go in any activity on a minute-to-minute basis. We can pray these breath prayers before getting out of bed, in traffic, making lunch, or in a class or meeting. These prayers can become powerful and peaceful additions to our prayer life as we seek to live in a continuous state of prayer like Jesus.

I love you, Jesus!
Come, Holy Spirit!
Jesus, My Savior!
Abba! Father!
My Lord and My God
I can do all things in Christ who strengthens me.
Please help me, Jesus!
Be not afraid.
Lord Jesus Christ, Son of God, have mercy on me, a sinner.
Guide me and lead me, O Holy Spirit.
Jesus, I trust in You!
Here I am, Lord. I come to do your will.
All Thee, none me.

Your breath prayer(s) can be anything you desire.

Love pours from the heart of the person filled with prayers for God's grace for themselves and others. There are times, though, that we all find ourselves in the desert experiencing dryness in prayer where we do not feel God is listening or answering. We must do our best not to get discouraged, to persevere in prayer, and to examine if we might be asserting our own will rather than praying for the grace to accept God's will. Pray, "Come, Holy Spirit!"

> If we do not fill our mind with prayer, it will fill itself with anxieties, worries, temptations, resentments, and unwelcome memories.
> —Scott Hahn, *Signs of Life* (2009, 91)

There are other instances when our prayer time is interrupted by mental distractions. In my experience, this frequently happens, even daily, as I think about it. You may find this also happens to you. Please don't let this be discouraging. It's normal. I once heard a priest say, "Do you think this upsets God? No! How pleased He is with you for all the times you fought off the distractions during your prayer session so you could lift your mind and heart back to Him."

Whatever you do, protect yourself from giving in to the temptation to stop praying. It will all come around. Stick with it because the Holy Spirit is interceding with and for you. By entering prayer with an attitude of: "If it is your will, Father, not my will," bring your needs, requests, desires, hopes, and dreams to God.

With a good understanding of the proper nutrients and prepared to provide the needed nourishment and a heart-healthy prayer diet, you're now ready to bear good fruit in the Body of Christ. You'll do this by developing your unique way of sharing and investing your God-given gifts and talents with those around you. Let's explore what this looks like in Chapter 11.

11
GOOD FRUIT

A good tree cannot bear bad fruit, nor can a rotten tree bear good fruit. Every tree that does not bear good fruit will be cut down and thrown into the fire. So by their fruits you will know them.
—Matthew 7:18–20

Love is a fruit in season at all times,
and within reach of every hand.
—St. Teresa of Calcutta

Pomegranate juice and seeds have been known to increase blood count, improve blood circulation, and may prevent hardening of the arteries.

Bear good fruit. This recurring Biblical theme is first introduced in the Old Testament and repeated consistently throughout the New Testament. Earlier, I gave examples of how specific personal gifts might be used to bear good fruit.

We will look more closely now at how your God-given gifts and talents can be used fruitfully in the Body of Christ by exploring practical suggestions that can help you cultivate ideas of your own, using these blessings from God to bear good fruit in the Body of Christ and keep Jesus alive in the world.

> The meaning of life is to find your gift. The purpose of life is to give it away.
> —Pablo Picasso

My career in finance took me to a downtown high rise every day, dressed in a suit and tie for many years. Naturally, I had to keep up with shining my shoes. I would do it myself early on until a resourceful shoe shiner established himself as a trustworthy person who got access to work in the building. Every week, he would work his way from floor to floor, stopping on our floor on Wednesdays.

Jerome was a pleasant man, quick with an infectious smile and laugh. A good-natured man, Jerome could work wonders on shoes, touching up even the most worn and scarred footwear. For his expertise in this trade, he earned the affectionate moniker "The Shoe Doctor" or simply Doctor.

Doctor was kind, but there was no mistaking he was there to make a living. We would often be so wrapped up in our work that we didn't notice he had arrived. You soon knew he was there when you would get a tap on the shoulder. With that tap, he wasn't inquiring if you needed a shoeshine; no, it was as if to say, "hand them over; you need a shine." Most everyone always obliged.

Over time, the Doctor built a rapport with each of his clients, learning how they liked their shoes shined, and was trusted to take a pair of shoes for a week if new soles were needed. Jerome had a bold black cross drawn on his shoeshine kit in magic marker, indicating he was a Christian.

Jerome and long-time employees at the firm where I worked aged together, for he worked our floor for more than a decade. He was our friend. One week, he told us his mother had died and that he didn't have a suit to wear to her funeral. Out of caring, several of us at the office chipped in to purchase Jerome a suit and shoes. He was appreciative.

Not long after this, Jerome stopped coming to the floor. Sadly, we learned that he had also passed away and felt honored that the suit we had purchased was also Jerome's funeral attire.

Jerome was blessed with a personality and demeanor that suited someone in his line of work. He took pride in his craft, had real attention to detail, and, combined with his trustworthiness and infectious laugh, was a pleasure to see each week. In doing his work, Jerome left others feeling good and looking sharp.

We grew to care for Jerome and enjoyed supporting his business, trying to tip generously so he was rewarded and recognized for his work. While this was not charity, taking opportunities to support each other in small ways builds treasure in heaven and strengthens us as members of the Body of Christ. Bear good fruit, even in small endeavors.

Share Your Gifts

Sharing our gifts entails someone giving of oneself and another receiving generously. It is an exchange that allows both the giver and receiver to participate in the act of sharing. Sometimes we are the giver, and sometimes we are on the receiving end. At other times, it can be a reciprocal opportunity, like my relationship with Jerome, with both sides giving and receiving.

God has endowed us with unique personalities, traits, and talents so we will use them to bear good fruit in a way that shares His love that is deep within us with others, glorifies Him, brings the light of Jesus into the world, and draws people together for the greater good in the Body of Christ.

God did not give our gifts to us to store them away and only use them for family and friends. No, He gave us our unique attributes to cultivate and display, using them to become instruments of His love, creativity, beauty, peace, and joy. God blessed us with all this, so, acting in unity with the Holy Spirit, we will attract others to Him through Jesus Christ.

> Let each of us please his neighbor for his good, to edify him.
> —Romans 15:2 (RSV-CE)

We cannot bear good fruit unless our hearts are in the right place. What follows is a short set of spiritual reminders that should bring our intentions and actions in closer alignment with the love and will of God:

1. As Jesus informed us, it all starts with the greatest commandments—to love God with your whole being and to love your neighbor as yourself (Matt. 25:37–39). Jesus said everything else "depends on these two commandments" and there is great and pure truth to this (v. 40). To bear good fruit, everything we do must be done for the love of God and the love of neighbor, not for selfish reasons.
2. Stay attached to the Vine. Live in the presence of Jesus. Abide in His love. Keep Christ as the reason

for everything you do if you hope to bear good fruit. Be Christ-centered and other people-centered, not self-centered, looking for recognition.
3. Invite the Holy Spirit to be awakened and alive in your heart, and then listen for what God wants you to do moment by moment. Imitate Jesus by responding to the promptings of the Holy Spirit. The Holy Spirit will guide your actions, so they bear good fruit in the Body of Christ.
4. We bear good fruit when we share God's love with others by using the personal gifts and talents He gives to us in a way that serves others, offers sacrificial love, and shares the burdens and joys of others. We bear good fruit when we do these things with a grateful and prayerful heart, in Jesus' name, praising God for the opportunity.

As each one has received a gift, use it to serve one another as good stewards of God's varied grace.
—1 Peter 4:10

I can't possibly place myself in your shoes or speak to how it would be best for you to share your gifts. Only you can do this. In Matthew Kelly's words, "Certainly we are each responsible for finding a way to express our unique abilities. It would be a mistake to abdicate that responsibility."[1]

I can offer suggestions relating to different personalities and traits to help you envision what you might do. As you do, ask Jesus what He wants you to do. Then take the first step.

> Take the first step in faith. You don't have to see the
> whole staircase, just take the first step.[2]
> —Martin Luther King Jr.

The first consideration is how to best share your gifts in building up the Church wherever you reside. Review all the ministries and programs offered in your local church and select those you feel will best allow you to be a good example and to share the light and love of Christ with others. Start or get involved with a new ministry using your strengths, gifts, and abilities.

Now let's look at possibilities to share your gifts with the People of God beyond the physical walls of your church building. If something here resonates with you, it is likely because certain passions inside you align well with the activity being described. Indeed, there is a good chance you are beginning to be inspired by the Holy Spirit!

On the other hand, if a suggestion feels uncomfortable to you, it could be because you have a mix of gifts that don't align well with that activity, or you may not have the resources. That's OK! It simply means other ideas are better suited for someone with your personality, skills, or in your stage of life.

> Take advantage of the abilities with which God has gifted
> you to further his Kingdom in some way.[3]
> —Pope Francis

Bearing Good Fruit with Your Gifts

❦ Pray. Anyone, everyone, anywhere and everywhere, can always lift their hearts and minds to God in prayers of blessing, adoration, petition, intercession, thanksgiving, and praise.

GOOD FRUIT

You may be: With any personality, character trait, value, and ability, one can always pray.

※ You help the elderly lady at the airport struggling with her luggage after picking it up from baggage claim. You share and "own" her burden by offering to walk with her to put her bags in the trunk of her car.

You may be: patient, loving, attentive, compassionate, committed, caring, concerned, considerate, empathetic, flexible, friendly, kind, personable, polite, selfless, strong.

※ After a flood in your town, you notice a couple you don't know has been forced to vacate their home and are living on their property in an old, beat-up trailer. Their wet furniture is on the curb for the next trash collection. You provide for them by dropping off a monetary gift for their needs.

You may be: caring, compassionate, decent, decisive, entrepreneurial, fair, generous, helpful, humble, kind, leader, merciful, observant, patriotic, principled, purposeful, resourceful, respectful, self-confident, secure, businesslike, determined, emotional, moralistic.

※ An elderly man is waiting five people behind you to use the public bathroom at a sporting event. Although you are four people from the urinal, you speak up for the man so he can go to the front of the line. Everyone else obliges.

You may be: adaptable, admirable, alert, bold, brave, candid, confident, concerned, considerate, courteous, dutiful, direct, hospitable, impressive, intuitive, leader, mature, observant.

🌿 You are a freshman in high school, and you've noticed one of your classmates repeatedly being unkind to another friend. You stick up for the friend being picked on, telling the other girl that her behavior is unacceptable; if it doesn't improve, she will no longer be considered a friend. She is in two classes with you and decides to no longer speak to you.

You may be: admirable, authentic, forthright, communicative, confident, compassionate, courageous, daring, devoted, dependable, equitable, frank, forgiving, genuine, good-natured, honest, loyal, mature, peaceful, persuasive, principled, reliable, ethical, supportive, tough.

🌿 You are a resident in an assisted living community. Walking down the hall one day, you notice an unfamiliar person sitting on a sofa by herself. You approach and introduce yourself to learn she is a new resident who has yet to meet anyone. You welcome and sit with her, and before long, you have been talking with your new friend for 45 minutes.

You may be: amiable, attentive, calm, caring, charming, colorful, companionly, dependable, dynamic, easygoing, faithful, friendly, gracious, interesting, leisurely, modest, neat, optimistic, sensitive, sociable, sincere, understanding.

🌿 You and your wife get a babysitter for date night twice a month, and you regularly go to a few local restaurants and taverns. You have gotten to know many of the regulars, all of whom are excited to see the two of you walk in because you have a genuine interest in the lives of others, and you always liven up the place.

You may be: affable, amiable, athletic, attractive, authentic, captivating, charismatic, cheerful, clever, deep, dependable, dynamic, energetic, exciting, faithful, feisty, friendly, fun-loving, funny, genuine, impressive, interested, kind, modest, personable, popular, relaxed, sincere.

🌿 You own a small business, employing 25 people and providing a valued service for the local economy and community. The company is also known for a culture of Christian values that are preserved internally and maintained in every customer interaction.

You may be: active, anticipative, bright, captivating, competent, decisive, disciplined, educated, energetic, fair, faithful, focused, hardworking, industrious, insightful, innovative, leader, passionate, positive, realistic, spiritual, steadfast, trustworthy.

🌿 You take two personal days from work to drive six hours to attend the viewing and funeral of the mother of a good friend and to support the family. After an overnight stay, you drive six hours home.

You may be: attentive, empathetic, sensitive, willing, generous, gracious, able, conscientious, selfless, considerate, dedicated, dependable, loving, sympathetic, principled, sentimental, thoughtful.

🌿 You were planning a quiet weekend at home. Looking through your email, you see a request for a volunteer at the local homeless shelter on Saturday night from 6 pm to 12 am. Instead of relaxing at home, you fill the inconvenient shift at the shelter by sitting with and conversing with the guests.

You may be: available, introverted, giving, discreet, diligent, flexible, helpful, hospitable, independent, merciful, non-judgmental, respectful, responsive, self-denying, spontaneous, uncomplaining, warm.

❦ An opportunity to go to the big game on Saturday is presented to you. That's the same day your nephew has scheduled to work on his Eagle Scout project with fellow scouts, and a deadline is looming. Knowing your skillful handiwork, he asks for your help. You sacrifice going to the game for the opportunity to help and support your nephew and his family.

You may be: enthusiastic, proactive, determined, handy, hardworking, skillful, problem-solver, selfless, competent, cooperative, mentorship, dedicated, creative, diligent, efficient, focused, dependable.

❦ You organize a 5K walk/run for a charitable cause.

You may be: athletic, enthusiastic, capable, organized, determined, leader, passionate, personable, sociable, popular, persuasive, inspiring.

❦ Recently retired and well-connected socially, you agree to lead a volunteer effort to clean up the shoreline in your area-playing your small part in beautifying God's creation.

You may be: driven, resourceful, responsible, collaborative, technological, punctual, open-minded, determined, diligent, imaginative, intuitive, organized, energetic, willing, purposeful, convincing, articulate.

🌿 A group of college Christians at your campus, of which you are a part, volunteer one Saturday each month to go into the local community to work at a food pantry for the needy and perform odd jobs for elderly neighbors.

You may be: sociable, adventurous, compassionate, athletic, confident, charitable, dedicated, good-natured, healthy, energetic, handy, giving, determined, hardworking, outgoing.

🌿 You go to your son's house to be with your large family at Thanksgiving. The place is swarming with your grandchildren who look forward to sitting with you to hear your stories about the past and of their ancestors. You take time to also share with them the wisdom you have collected over your 87 years.

You may be: accessible, affectionate, loving, clear-headed, alert, attentive, captivating, cheerful, colorful, devoted, easygoing, eloquent, gentle, peaceful, patient, generous, gracious, funny, lively, lovable, observant, relaxed, sentimental, warm, wise.

> They shall bear fruit even in old age.
> —Psalm 92:15

This list of ideas and corresponding personal gifts is in no way exhaustive. Some of these actions take little effort; others are more involved. I'll discuss this more specifically in the next chapter. It matters not what you do with your gifts provided it is for the love of God and neighbor.

Note that these examples are for people in various stages of life. Our gifts evolve throughout our lives as God blesses us with what is needed to play the part He has in mind for us at a particular time. To live aligned with God's will, we need to take an inventory of our gifts periodically so we can be open to and understand what the Holy Spirit is putting on our heart and mind to do, perform, and accomplish.

Keep the short yet powerful and spiritually significant checklist at the forefront of your endeavors. As long as you use the personal gifts in a way that 1) is done for the love of God and the love of neighbor, 2) keeps Jesus Christ at the center of your life and the reason for everything you do, 3) is responsive to the prompting of the Holy Spirit, allowing Him to guide your actions, and 4) humbly serves others, offers sacrificial and inconveniencing love, and shares the burdens and joys of others, then your efforts should bear good fruit and attract others to God through the light and face of Jesus Christ that shines through you.

> Let us not grow tired of doing good, for in due time we shall reap our harvest, if we do not give up. So then, while we have the opportunity, let us do good to all, but especially to those who belong to the family of the faith.
> —Galatians 6:9–10

INVEST YOUR TALENTS

The traditionally accepted message from Jesus in the parable of the talents is that we must invest our God-given talents responsibly to bring a return on that investment to the Lord. Paraphrasing the notes to Matthew 25:14 (NABRE), if you use your talents faithfully, you will enjoy eternal life in heaven; if you are lazy and inactive with your talents, you will be excluded from heaven. If this isn't a call to action, what is?

The return we should pursue is to be generous in bearing good fruit with our talents similar to what is expected with our personal gifts. That is, to use them in a way that gives God the glory, shares His love in our souls with others and lets them see and be attracted to the light and face of Jesus through the Holy Spirit, who is present in our hearts.

While our personal gifts are intangible, when we let them shine, and the fruit of the Holy Spirit (love, joy, peace, etc.) becomes more evident as we grow in Christ, the product becomes the visible action described in the previous list.

Recall that a talent is something you do exceptionally well, something that others might struggle to do, and an ability you have perfected over time with much training and focus. Our talents are tangible. They are improved when exhibited with specific personal gifts that bring out the best of our skills. For example, you might be a good guitar player and singer, yet your personality makes those talents shine. Both are gifts from God that we should use to glorify Him, attract others to Christ, and build up the Church, the Body of Christ.

Is there something you have the desire to learn? Do it! Don't keep putting it off. The desire in you could be the Holy Spirit guiding you there because God has something He wants to accomplish through you with this interest and soon-to-be newly discovered talent.

> A Christian who withdraws into himself, hiding all that the Lord has given him, is not a Christian! I would ask the many young people present to be generous with their God-given talents for the good of others, the Church and our world.[4]
>
> —Pope Francis

What are your talents, and how are you using them?

First and foremost, as with your personal gifts, seek ways to use your talents in your church. Here are some ideas:

Join the choir if you are a good singer.

Join the music ministry if you play an instrument.

Join the Finance Committee if you are good with numbers or a CPA.

Join the Long-Term Planning Committee if you have vision.

Be a lector/reader at any age if you are a good orator or aspire to be.

Lead the teen group if you interact well with that age group.

Take a leadership role with your teen peers because you are a bright light for others your age.

Display your youthful zeal for your faith and church within your social circle.

Be a Catechist/Sunday school teacher if you have that talent.

Volunteer your time, talent, and treasure to help raise money or to reach those in need.

Publish a monthly newsletter or a faith-based book if you are a writer.

Upgrade or manage the technology or live streaming capabilities if you have that skill.

Support church-related charitable causes according to the means your vocation has provided.

Design and print a church pamphlet if you are a graphic designer.

Paint a mural on the walls of the church Hall depicting the life of Christ if you are an artist.

The opportunities are endless, really, and the rewards for the kingdom of God are great. The objective is to volunteer to use your talents to keep people coming and attract lapsed and new members because they can see the face and love of Jesus Christ alive where you worship.

Not only should we invest our talents to benefit our local church, but we also need to be generous with our talents "for the good of others, the Church and our world" as Pope Francis stated in the previous quote. We must also use them in other ways to bear good fruit in the Body of Christ.

You listed your top talents in Chapter 4. Other talents may just be surfacing, and others may be revealed later in life. Embrace them and pray for the Holy Spirit's guidance on how Jesus would like you to use them. The answers will come, and the opportunities to be a shining light for Christ will open for you as you polish these talents and make yourself available to use them as He thinks would be best in God's grand plan. It may necessitate moving outside your comfort zone or displaying your talent in a new way. Scripture recorded God, the Father and the Son, repeatedly encouraging the prophets, the disciples, and you and me to "Be not afraid."

Avoid selling yourself short. You don't need to be on a stage, on an athletic field of play, the smartest in the class, presiding over a courtroom, preaching from a pulpit, or performing surgery to have a talent. Sure, those who do these things are talented. You are too, and your talents might include:

gardening	social media	fishing	magic	boat detailing
bartender	coaching	friendship	quick-witted	encouragement
embroidering	surfing	mentoring	sales	listening
cooking	coloring	skateboarding	photography	softball
parenting	dog-sitting	storytelling	investing	history
cleaning windows	flower displays	wrapping gifts	serving tables	playing cards
using tools	mechanic	marketing	word processing	housekeeping
humor	butcher	woodworking	teaching	golf
math	finance	coding	nursing	home decor
public speaking	caregiver	fitness	gaming	travel planning

> Willingness to give ourselves out of love, even if it entails suffering, is what makes us fruitful.[5]
> —Scott Hahn: *A Father Who Keeps His Promises*

It is up to you and the Holy Spirit to determine how you will share your gifts and invest your talents for the Body of Christ and the world around you. Whatever you decide to do with these God-given gifts, be creative and original, have confidence, find a niche, teach others, act with integrity and character, show others the goodness in you and see the goodness in others that is Jesus Christ, do it for the love of God and neighbor, look people in the eye and listen attentively, be fully present in the moment, include your audience if you have one, engage with your customers, be merciful and understanding when things don't go as planned, and enjoy yourself. When you enjoy yourself, you exude the Spirit, radiate the love, and reflect the light of Jesus Christ.

Use your talents to reach others, teach others, entertain others, spread joy and happiness, lead others, give others opportunities they may otherwise not have, inspire others, or move others to ponder the truths of our faith.

You will bear good fruit when you conduct yourself in this manner as you share gifts and invest talents. Glorify the Lord, our God by returning your gifts and talents to Him through others. Remember, the kingdom of God is at hand, your hand—extend it dutifully and joyfully to those you encounter through your gifts and talents, and give God praise and thanksgiving for the opportunities.

> Let us be what we are, and be that well, so that we may bring honor to the Master Craftsman whose handiwork we are.[6]
> —St. Francis de Sales

> The fruit of faith should be evident in our lives, for being a Christian is more than making sound professions of faith. It should reveal itself in practical and visible ways.
> —St. Ignatius of Antioch

Now that we have seen how different personal gifts and talents could align with practical activities, you may ponder how your unique collection can be fruitfully shared and invested. It doesn't matter how simple or extravagant is the action you take. Every bit of it can bear fruit in the Body of Christ. We will now consider in Chapter 12 that any action we take—both little things and greater callings—will be pleasing to God and effective in building up the Body of Christ in our community and the world when we do it with great love.

12
LITTLE GREATNESS

A little yeast leavens the whole batch of dough.
—Galatians 5:9

Great things are done by a series of small things brought together.
—Vincent Van Gogh

In frigid temperatures, additional blood is sent to the small vessels in the nose; this helps heat the air to body temperature in the little time it takes to arrive at the lungs.

Marie-Francoise-Thérèse Martin was the youngest of nine children, born so frail and fragile that her doctors and parents were concerned for her life. The little infant was a fighter who surprisingly grew stronger and survived. She was the youngest child, she was the favorite, and she was spoiled. She was also an active child and a handful, becoming playfully prankish and stubborn. Notably, her temper would get the best of her, and she would have theatrical outbursts. Thérèse Martin was also an unsettlingly clever little girl.

Living in France, her parents raised their children in a Christian family, regularly praying and reading Scripture together and learning the importance of performing good deeds. Her spirituality blossomed early; she even said she wanted to be a nun when she was only three. As she grew older, she was filled with an impassioned love for Jesus and a deep desire to serve and suffer for Him.

Thérèse suffered greatly into her teens, often in tears. Her mother died when she was four, she endured painful illnesses and developed depression, anxiety, and self-doubt. Two of her sisters preceded Thérèse into the Carmelite Monastery, one of whom cared for her as a mother. She was distraught without them.

At thirteen, God blessed her with a complete conversion of her soul that instantly moved her from her affliction with depression, anxiety, and insecurity to being filled with charity, calmness, selflessness, internal strength, and the joy that she had lost after her mother died. She petitioned to join the Monastery several times, first at ten, getting turned away each time until the age of fifteen.

Thérèse loved nature and flowers, humbly considering herself not a rose but like the little wildflowers in a field or forest. Translated from her autobiography, *Story of a Soul* (1898), she understood "if all flowers wanted to be roses nature would lose her springtime beauty, and the fields would no longer be decked out with little wildflowers. So it is in the world of souls, Jesus' garden." She embraced her littleness, humbly referred to herself as The Little Flower of Jesus, and lived a hidden and simple life yet was perpetually in bloom, glorifying God in small and ordinary ways.

Thérèse had childlike trust, faith, hope, and love for Jesus. This humble, childlike piety and her deep spirituality, manifest in her simple, small, and ordinary actions done with love, defined the self-professed "little way" to be a saint and to get to heaven for this young woman who died in 1897 at the age of twenty-four. In 1925, she became known as Saint Thérèse of Lisieux.[1]

To get a sense of the little way, a few of the things Thérèse of Lisieux noted doing included controlling her temper by simply smiling when the often cantankerous elderly nuns would criticize or have a harsh word for her, helping the same nuns walk around the convent while being pleasant and biting her tongue, showing patience during group prayer for the annoyingly noisy habits of some of the other sisters, and even folding a napkin with great intention and love while offering her work to God. Small things like this done with great love build up the kingdom of God far better than larger deeds done to receive praise and glory for oneself, out of pride, or because we were expected to do it.

> Remember that nothing is small in the eyes of God. Do all that you do with love.
> —St. Thérèse of Lisieux

SMALL THINGS

The blood cells march through the capillaries in single-file formation, playing their individual part in the human body. During their short life span, they follow the mundane pattern of circulation over and over, awaiting the call to spring into action. In a healthy body, about all the blood cells can expect to help beyond the normal blood flow are the small things. Platelets move in to stop bleeding caused by minor cuts or abrasions. White blood cells fight infection and absorb red blood cells that leak from damaged capillaries to cause bruising. After the blood clots, red blood cells and platelets move to damaged areas and, with collagen, build new tissue that closes a wound, leaving a scar.

For the Body of Christ, the small things we may attend to might involve a positive change in our attitude, a minor automobile accident, an upset family member, others at church, a houseguest, a neighbor needing help, or a stranger on a sidewalk. The observant Christian will notice these things as opportunities and, like a blood cell in the human body, will take ordinary and small action at the prompting of the Holy Spirit to fulfill God's will in that moment with humility and love. The ob*servant* one is always alert for servant opportunities. Often the simple and ordinary require spontaneity or come to mind in an instant.

hold open the door	offer a compliment	tip a little extra
send short handwritten notes	help a child to do something	bring your co-worker coffee
say hi to a stranger	surprise your neighbor by cutting their grass	turn the other cheek

Anjezë Gonxhe Bojaxhiu was a disciple of St. Thérèse of Lisieux. Upon entering her first convent in India, she wanted to take the Saint's name when she took her first vows. Because another nun already had done this, she settled for Teresa and later became the missionary we know as Mother Teresa (St. Teresa of Calcutta). She also followed the little way of Thérèse of Lisieux, and when she spoke, Mother Teresa echoed the recurring theme she learned from studying The Little Flower of Jesus. These two quotes attributed to Mother Teresa could easily have flowed from the lips of her spiritual guide.

Do ordinary things with extraordinary love.[2]
—St. Teresa of Calcutta

It is not the magnitude of our actions but the amount of love that is put into them that matters.
—St. Teresa of Calcutta

It's the small things that matter. It sounds like a cliché yet it's a powerful and true principle when you consider every artist's painting begins with the first brushstroke, a sports team's success starts on the first day of practice, a vehicle purrs down the highway because the oil is changed, the beauty of a pianist's recital relies on the intricate tuning of the instrument, and a student advances through school by completing daily assignments.

On what does the success of these examples and anything worth pursuing depend? Attention to detail—the ordinary and small things. And so it is in building up the Body of Christ.

> For the body does not consist of one member, but of many…But God has so composed the body, giving the greater honor to the inferior part, that there may be no discord in the body, but that the members may have the same care for one another. If one member suffers, all suffer together; if one member is honored, all rejoice together.
> —1 Corinthians 12:14, 24–26 (RSV-CE)

What we do or overlook doing affects the entire Body of Christ "so that what each one does or suffers in and for Christ bears fruit for all."[3] To build up this Body, we are to share love and joy wherever we can.

share in someone's suffering	give flowers unexpectedly	put extra in the poor box
talk with the homeless man;	do chores without being asked	buy someone's meal
look him in the eye; ask his name	lend a helping hand	give blood

Hospitality covers a lot of ground in building up the Body of Christ. There are a few differently worded definitions of the word online. The one I like best is this from Dictionary.com "the quality or disposition of receiving guests or strangers in a warm, friendly, generous way." The Christian family is called to be hospitable to guests, strangers, visitors, those in need, friends, family, and even those with which we may not get along.

We see examples of and references to hospitality throughout the Bible. God, who is all love, got it started with His creation and soon after by accommodating Adam and Eve with the Garden of Eden and all they needed. His creation has sustained people from Adam and Eve to the time of Jesus and in the 2000 years since He lived on this earth. God is divinely and eternally hospitable.

During the life of Jesus, the innkeeper offered hospitality to Mary and Joseph by letting them use the stable for His birth. During the public ministry of Jesus, He was always invited in for a place to stay and food to eat as He traversed the land from Galilee to Judea. Many of His parables taught hospitality, among many other lessons. The miracle at the wedding feast at Cana exhibited hospitality, and Jesus often refers to banquets and extends invitations to join them.

The root of hospitality is love, for Jesus commanded us to "love one another as I love you" (John 15:12), to "love your neighbor as yourself" (Matt. 22:39), and to feed the hungry, give the thirsty a drink, welcome the stranger, clothe the naked, care for the sick, and visit those in prison (Matt. 25:35–36). Jesus also taught whatever you do for the least of my brothers, you do for me (Matt. 25:40). Jesus suggests hospitality should extend beyond the home and the church into the community.

> Above all hold unfailing love for one another, since love covers a multitude of sins. Practice hospitality ungrudgingly to one another.
> —1 Peter 4:9 (RSV-CE)

> Do not neglect hospitality, for through it some have unknowingly entertained angels.
> —Hebrews 13:2

welcome the stranger	visit the elderly in a nursing home	receive your guests selflessly
talk with the wallflower	offer your coat on a winter night	ask if anyone needs anything
invite the outcast	let a stranger walk under your umbrella	introduce strangers

Doing small and ordinary things with great love for God and neighbor doesn't need to involve sharing our gifts and talents, although it can. As the fruit of the Holy Spirit ripens in us, we will likely begin to look for and notice opportunities all around. When we keep Jesus' words "that you do unto me" in mind and on our hearts, we will see the goodness who is Jesus in others—friend, family, stranger, and foe—and will recognize the best way to share God's love and joy in that moment. Understand what little you do is looked upon as greatness from up above. Realize when you do something, the person receiving it may have just prayed for that. Be the answer sent by God. A small gesture may mean the world to someone else. Be a small miracle for that someone today.

be present, and listen	allow your teen to teach you	call your grandparent
say please, sorry, thank-you	pick up litter in the parking lot	smile, always smile
compromise	show interest in a friend's life	speak kind words
give benefit of the doubt	remember to ask how it went	be a true friend
give to the beggar	generate laughter	encourage others

What you give to the beggar is between you and God. What the beggar does with what you give is between God and the beggar.

> Pleasant words are like a honeycomb, sweetness to the soul and health to the body.
> —Proverbs 16:24 (RSV-CE)

> Every time you smile at someone, it is an action of love, a gift to that person, a beautiful thing.
> —St. Teresa of Calcutta

> A friend loves at all times.
> —Proverbs 17:17 (RSV-CE)

When endorphins and other hormones release in the brain, they help reduce the feeling of pain, help people cope with stress, lower blood pressure, increase energy, lessen anxiety and depression, and boost self-esteem. The release of these neurochemicals can be enhanced by exercise, laughter, meditation, eating and drinking, helping others, and acts of kindness. When this happens, it produces positive feelings and a sense of joy. What a wonderful parallel this is to the good that we do and the love and joy that we spread every day in the Body of Christ at the direction of Jesus and carried out in unity with the Holy Spirit. The effect this has on the entire Body is uplifting.

Greater Callings

More severe attacks require more attention and greater velocity from the blood cells as they rush toward an incident like a buildup of plaque in the veins or a total blockage that causes a heart attack. The same can be said for the members of the Body of Christ who throw caution to the wind and respond without personal concern to a house fire, a natural disaster, a terrorist strike, or a major accident.

When a cardiac event occurs in the human body, new capillaries and arteries can form to keep blood and oxygen flowing to the extremities. The same can be said for the Body of Christ, where major trauma stirs widespread sorrow and sympathy and inspires in some a determined desire to help tangibly after the initial shock subsides. This desire is the working of the Holy Spirit, leading chosen Christians to greater callings.

> I was travelling by train to Darjeeling when I heard the voice of God. I was sure it was God's voice. I was certain He was calling me to something more. The message was clear.
>
> —St. Teresa of Calcutta

These greater callings open new avenues of love and service in the Body of Christ. One might lead an effort to collect clothing and other necessities for the family displaced by the house fire. Another family might open their home to their traumatized neighbors. After a natural disaster, we always see individuals or groups of people descend on the area with donated provisions, emotional support for those impacted, and the energy and skill to help clear or rebuild the area.

Prayer chains get activated around the world. Affluent people or notable role models establish foundations or non-profits to aid those affected by the disaster. Often, these organizations remain open and funded to provide aid in future disasters. After 9/11, corporate, independent, and family foundations that had already been established donated billions to the relief and recovery efforts, according to The Foundation Center.[4] There is a greater sense of unity, love, and humility that develops in the aftermath of these major events, all at the inspiration of the Holy Spirit.

Greater callings also occur absent these "cardiac" events. One person is inspired to establish a non-profit for the needy in the community. Over time, that effort develops into a homeless shelter, a food pantry, and a thrift store organized to provide support the organization financially. In time, the non-profit regularly feeds hundreds of families, employs 20 people, and provides numerous volunteering opportunities in the community.

Musically gifted, you and your friends form a garage band that plays several genres, including contemporary Christian music. Soon enough, you are writing your lyrics, guided by the Holy Spirit. A Christian/Worship music station notices a demo of a few of your songs, and you hear one of them on the airwaves. Your fanbase grows.

Don't be surprised when something you start and view as small begins to gain traction or momentum and grows to a level that far surpasses your imagination. When what you do aligns with God's will, and you step into it with all trust and confidence in the Lord, great things can happen. When you do it with a profound love of God with your whole being and with love for your neighbor, you will bear good fruit and build up the Body of Christ.

> For my thoughts are not your thoughts, neither are your ways my ways, says the Lord. For as the heavens are higher than the earth, so are my ways higher than your ways and my thoughts than your thoughts.
> —Isaiah 55:8–9

> [God] who by the power at work within us is able to do far more abundantly than all we ask or think.
> —Ephesians 3:30

> Miss no single opportunity of making some small sacrifice, here by a smiling look, there by a kindly word; always doing the smallest right and doing it all for love.
> —St. Thérèse of Lisieux

Having just completed Part 3, you are now equipped with an understanding of the spiritual necessities needed to play your part in the Body of Christ. You should also have a better idea of how you might cultivate your unique God-given gifts and talents to glorify God by keeping Jesus Christ alive in the world.

As you trust and act, it is important to know that you have not been sent forth on your own to build up this Body.

Yes, you will certainly need to be in the proper shape to love God and neighbor and to carry Jesus with you wherever you go and in whatever you do. However, you won't be in this alone. As you will see in Part 4, it will be a collaboration.

PART 4

Collaboration

After this the Lord appointed seventy[-two] others, and sent them on ahead of him, two by two, into every town and place where he himself was about to come.
—Luke 10:1 (RSV-CE)

No one should follow what he considers to be good for himself, but rather what seems good for another. Let them put Christ before all else; and may he lead us all to everlasting life.
—St. Benedict, *Rule of Saint Benedict*

One pint of donated blood can save up to three lives.
—givingblood.org

13
AS YOURSELF

You shall love your neighbor as yourself.
—Matthew 22:39, Mark 12:31

My son, be attentive to my words; incline your ear to my sayings. Let them not escape from your sight; keep them within your heart. For they are life to him who finds them, and healing to all his flesh. Keep your heart with all vigilance; for from it flow the springs of life.
—Proverbs 4:20–23

How can one love self without being selfish? How can one love others without losing self? The answer is: By loving both self and neighbor in God. It is his love that makes us love both self and neighbor rightly.
—Fulton J. Sheen, *Three to Get Married*

Jesus chose not to send His apostles and other disciples to be His witnesses on their own. They were sent two by two. He wanted it to be a collaborative effort, each having a partner as they moved around. Sure, it's possible in some areas, they split up to reach more people, reconvening when necessary and before moving on. Later, the apostle Paul traveled with companions or called for them to join him (including Barnabas, Timothy, John Mark, Silas, and Luke).

Expanding on this theme of collaboration, Jesus not only wants us to work together, but He also gave the all-encompassing greatest commandments to His early followers and every Christian since to love God with all our being and to "love your neighbor as yourself." Just before His ascension, he also told them, "you will receive power when the Holy Spirit comes upon you, and you will be my witnesses...to the ends of the earth" (Acts 1:8). In essence, Jesus was telling them to trust, listen to, and follow the promptings of the Holy Spirit. This collaborative effort allowed the apostles and first-century disciples to be most effective in helping build up the early Church. It was the model then, and it remains the model today. When followed with Christ-centered purpose, it allows us to be productive playing our part in building up the Body of Christ.

In Part 4, we will explore the three principles of this collaboration, beginning with the instruction to love yourself, which is fundamental to the second greatest commandment. This divine directive is emphasized repeatedly in the Bible, including by God the Father in the Old Testament. Jesus also does it in the gospels when He reveals this as the second greatest commandment. Finally, this teaching is reinforced three times by the apostles Paul and James.[1]

Love your neighbor *as yourself*. The last two words of this second greatest commandment have been the source of much attention, writing, and debate by Christian bishops, pastors, theologians, and the faithful down through the generations. These words also tend to get lost when the greatest two commandments are summarized with direct simplicity as love God and love your neighbor.

A search online finds numerous philosophical writings that discuss what Jesus means by "as yourself" and the contradictions between love—willing the good of the other for the other's sake, giving of and emptying oneself for the love and benefit of another person—and loving your neighbor as yourself. I will leave it to those with advanced degrees to argue the teachings of respected philosophers and theologians like St. Ignatius of Loyola, St. Augustine, St. Thomas Aquinas, and others on what Jesus meant when he said to love your neighbor as yourself.

In 1 John 4:7-21 (RSV-CE), the Gospel writer wrote again that God is love; he loves us so much that he sent His only Son into the world to die for us to save us from our sins and to rise from the dead so that we may have eternal life through Christ. John also said, "if God so loved us, we also ought to love one another" (v. 11). Later in the passage, he reminds us, "We love, because he first loved us" (v. 19).

God loves us. God is the original, unconditional, and everlasting love for all His children. To strive to love as God loves, we must love one another as He loves us, we must love ourselves because He does, and we must love our neighbor as we love ourselves. This goes hand in hand with the Golden Rule: to do unto others as you would have them do unto you (Matt. 7:12, Luke 6:31).

> He who desires to be good to others should not also be bad to himself.[2]
>
> —St. Ignatius of Loyola

When we love ourselves in a way that brings us closer to God, we can better share His love with others. As our relationship with the Father, the Son, and the Holy Spirit grows in intimacy, our love for ourselves and our lives will become more Christ-like. The more Christ-like this love is, the more it will be readily displayed in our thoughts, words, and actions toward our neighbor.

Some might be thinking but wait a minute—Jesus tells us to deny ourselves![3] He does, although the meaning of this is "to disown oneself as the center of one's existence" (notes to Matt. 16:24, [NABRE]). To deny ourselves is to resist being self-centered, prideful, or egotistical. To deny ourselves is to be Christ-centered and other-people centered. When we can do this, we live a servant's life with humility and love as Jesus loves.

After the meal at the Last Supper, in His last act of humility and service before His Passion and death on the cross, Jesus washed His apostle's feet and told them they must do the same. Jesus gave this as an example of how we are to love one another as he loves us. To love as he loves, we must also love ourselves in a self-denying, faithful, Christ-like manner. In this way, love of self as humble servant is a precondition for loving one another.

An important aspect of loving ourselves is caring for our well-being, i.e., mental (thinking), emotional (expressing), spiritual, physical, and relational. To be healthy in mind, body, and soul, it is our responsibility to care for ourselves holistically because letting one dimension of our well-being suffer tends to affect the other dimensions negatively. We should also attend to the small details like our habits, lifestyle, and nutrition. Each of these factors impacts how we feel about ourselves, determines our level of energy or stress, and influences our ability and desire to love (and help) our neighbor as Jesus asks of us.

I know this to be true. I experienced this firsthand, struggling with general anxiety disorder from a young age into adulthood. It manifested in a persistent feeling of nervousness within, that of butterflies and knots in my stomach that would intensify when faced with certain situations that I feared would inflict on me emotional or physical harm.

Because of these unfounded feelings and thoughts, I was reluctant to face such situations. I became imprisoned in my mind. Professionally, I pushed through the anxiety and did what I needed to do. Socially, I resisted. Into my 40s, and with a great deal of prayer for healing, I was introduced to a new term I had not heard before: social anxiety disorder. Finally, what I was suffering had a name, and I was relieved to learn I could defeat with professional help.

If you are reading this book and you suffer from any mental or emotional difficulties, I would like to impart this: it is the strong who ask for help. Friend, one is not weak who seeks professional help. By the grace of God, Jesus answered my prayers by bringing a wonderful therapist into my life who helped me to overcome this disorder. Through her, God freed me from this discordant cycle so I could love myself better and blossom into the person God designed me to be.

> Pray, hope, and don't worry. Worry is useless. God is merciful and will hear your prayer.[4]
> —St. Pio of Pietrelcina

To cope with my anxiety, I engaged in an unhealthy lifestyle and habits that were the antithesis of loving myself. Do you see how this works? As one dimension of our well-being slips or suffers, it can have a negative effect on others. In my former frame of mind and body, my love of self was damaged, and my ability to love my neighbor as Jesus wanted me to love was also held back. Thankfully, I had an intense yearning to be healed and the willingness to turn it over to God.

There is no one-size-fits-all solution related to caring for and loving ourselves. I do not presume to know where you are mentally, emotionally, spiritually, physically, and relationally. Only you can make an honest assessment of your well-being, and only you can choose to address the areas where you would like to feel better and improve. This is part of loving yourself. As you feel better, you'll be more inclined to share that love with others.

Please know I'm not insinuating that all can be of perfect health in each of these areas, much less that we're able to address and heal ourselves of all our afflictions on our own. We can seek help, however. I am also not implying that those suffering like this don't love themselves. If we are wounded in our well-being, we aren't at peak mental or physical capacity to love our neighbor. When we feel better in all areas, our ability to love our neighbor grows. When we love ourselves as God loves us, we will look to fix those areas of our life that may be holding us back.

As we age and our bodies begin to show it, we may need to alter our approaches toward loving our neighbor. We may become more prayerful for them or more inclined to cook a meal or take them some baked goods rather than helping them physically. We could send a note of love and encouragement. If you are still able, you may volunteer in some way. Those stricken with a debilitating illness, young or old, may just need to be the recipient of a neighbor's love and care. This is equally as important for the well-being of the Body of Christ.

If you don't feel well in one area, how you feel about yourself can negatively impact the love you can show your neighbor. Think about it. When we are physically fit for our age and frame, we have more energy, our emotional state tends to be more positive, and we feel better about ourselves. This should put us in a better frame of mind to treat our neighbor with love, in a better disposition to physically help our neighbor, and in a better emotional state to be there for our neighbor when in need. Alternatively, if we are in an unhealthy relationship, our emotions will suffer, and we may not be emotionally available to love our neighbor. The way you feel about yourself can lift others, or it may drag them down.

> The glory of God is man fully alive [in Him].
> —St. Irenaeus

Our spiritual health, that of the soul, must also be nourished.

The soul "refers to the innermost aspect of man, that which is of greatest value in him, that by which he is most especially in God's image ... The human body shares in the dignity of 'the image of God': it is a human body precisely because it is animated by a spiritual soul, and it is the whole human person that is intended to become, in the body of Christ, a temple of the Spirit ... it is because of its spiritual soul that the body made of matter becomes a living, human body; spirit and matter, in man, are not two natures united, but rather their union forms a single nature" (CCC 363-365).

I believe the wellness of our soul is even more important than that of mind and body "precisely because" it animates the human body and guides the whole person toward God. Our mind and body will not be properly animated if the soul is unwell. If the soul is sick, the shadow of darkness may have come upon us. For the soul to be afflicted, temptation and sin have infected our body, and sickened the Body of Christ. Therefore, our spiritual wellness is crucial for our love of self, our love of neighbor, and our love of God, and it is why loving ourselves is pivotal to being spiritually well.

As descendants of Adam and Eve living in a fallen world, we are always susceptible to temptation and the disease of sin. The Devil preys on the spiritual and physical weakness of every member of the Body of Christ, tempting each one to succumb to the infectious disease of sin and evil. When our body and soul give in to this infection, the entire Body of Christ is affected just as a biological illness spreads throughout a school, into families, and through the community. When one member of the Body of Christ suffers, we all suffer (1 Cor. 12:26). When I am involved in sin, I risk pulling in others, tempting others, and leading others to sin by my example. The same goes for the friends I keep and the risk of sin to which I may expose myself.

Like the white blood cells in the human body, Christians are the army of defense against the tempting attacks of Satan in the Body of Christ. The Devil cannot force us to sin. Instead, it is our free will to either ignore and resist Satan's temptation or to take the bait and engage in sinfulness. Even St. Paul admitted, "I do not do the good I want, but I do the evil I do not want" (Romans 7:19).

Thankfully, by the grace of God, we have spiritual reinforcement for protection against the evil one, but only if we fortify our souls before, during, and after temptation. In other words, like a regiment preparing for battle, we must always be alert to the threat of temptation and constantly call on the name of Jesus for His protection against the snares of the enemy.

St. Paul listed the spiritual weapons available to the army of the faithful in his letter to the Ephesians (6:10–20): the armor of *God*, loins girded in *truth*, the breastplate of *righteousness*, the equipment of *the gospel of peace*, the shield of *faith*, the helmet of *salvation,* and the sword of *the Spirit-the word of God.*

In a practical sense, how can we care for, protect, and defend the well-being and good health of our souls?

> But he bestows a greater grace; therefore, it says: "God resists the proud, but gives grace to the humble." So submit yourselves to God. Resist the Devil, and he will flee from you.
>
> —James 4:6–7

❦ As the apostle Paul wrote, "Pray without ceasing" (1 Thess. 5:17). The Most Holy Name of Jesus means God Saves. Cry out for Jesus when tempted, and trust and believe that He, who has already defeated sin and evil, will protect and save you. Prayer is our protection.

> Trust in the Lord with all your heart, and on your own intelligence do not rely; In all your ways be mindful of him, and he will make straight your paths.
>
> —Proverbs 3:5–6

❦ Avoid anything that might lead to sin. I know, this one isn't easy. Temptation is all around us—in social media, advertisements, movies, entertainment, and in what we stream. It's everywhere. It's in what we read, at establishments we frequent, and in the immodesty we see at pools and beaches. It may be in the habits of the people with whom we hang out. It is rooted in life. So how do we avoid it?

- Practice the Fruit of Self Control – if you find yourself tempted in certain situations, recognize it, and remove yourself from them until you master the self-control needed to protect yourself. For example, if your friends at school are heading down an unhealthy path, encourage them to reconsider. If they continue in that direction, be willing to let them go. It's hard, I know, but do not fear. Trust that you will make new friends who share your morals.

  If you find yourself having a wandering eye at the beach with your spouse or having lustful thoughts in another setting, recognize it, commit to resisting these temptations, move your chair to a different line of sight, and say a quick prayer asking the Holy Spirit to strengthen you. If the series you've been streaming has gotten a bit too raunchy, turn your head or leave the room until the scene is over, or maybe just let it go because more of the same is likely to come. When we practice self-control, it soon becomes second nature. Our conscience becomes more alert and aware of when we've entered a potentially harmful situation for the body and soul.

He asked us to be meek and humble of heart so we would find rest for our souls; the serenity that is the fruit of that self-control becomes the envy of the world.[5]

—Mother Angelica,
Mother Angelica on Suffering and Burnout

- Choose your words delicately. Our words are powerful. Be careful what you say and how you say it. Our words can be a blessing, or they can cut right through someone like a knife. Throughout my life, I have said things to get a laugh without considering the sensitivity of the person who was the subject of my words. For this, I am deeply sorry. Life is a process, and I've learned to be more sensitive to the feelings of others before I speak. Alternatively, our internal words, how we talk to ourselves, can be positive, supportive, and build us up, or they can be harmful, destructive, and tear us down.

Set a guard over my mouth, O Lord, keep watch over the door of my lips!
—Psalm 141:3 (RSV-CE)

- Sin and sinfulness are contagious. If we find that some in our circle of friends habitually engage in words, actions, or behaviors that are not of God, the soul begs us to distance ourselves from them. Gossip, for example, shows up unexpectedly in casual conversation. One person initiates it, and before we even know it, we and others enter the conversation to voice our opinions. Suddenly, a healthy conversation between friends falls off the rails. It happens so easily and normally that we don't even recognize that it's gossip until it's too late, if at all. The reputation of the person who is the subject of the critical barbs is wounded, if not damaged. Pope Francis tells us:

> The disease of gossiping, grumbling, and backbiting.... It is the disease of cowardly persons

who lack the courage to speak out directly, but instead speak behind other people's backs.... let us be on guard against the terrorism of gossip![6]

❦ Seek pastoral help and guidance. When facing temptation or when you've fallen into sin, turn to your pastor, minister, priest, or deacon for prayer, to draw strength and understanding in the Word of God, and to confess your faults and repent. The process of repentance is often misunderstood. For many, the word has connotations of punishment and pain. Repentance is an act of humility and deep contrition and remorse for your actions. To repent is to change, to walk in the right direction, to put on a new mind, to turn from sin and turn, 180 degrees if you will, to God. Ask for forgiveness and commit to change for the better.

❦ Live a virtuous life. Pray to increase in faith, hope, and love. Pray for help cleansing yourself of your idols (anything that controls your focus, turning your attention away from God), emptying out your vices, and extinguishing all lustful desires.

I realize what I just suggested sounds like a dull life. Did you know many of the saints faced the daily battle, just as we do? They strived to change for the better and persevered, turning their lives around to live this new way of serving God and neighbor. And you know what? They became the happiest people on Earth (all saints, not only those recognized as having heroic virtue). They were filled with abundant joy, peace, and love for God and neighbor. When our attention turns to worldly things, possessions, pleasures, power, and honor—all drawing our attention away from God—our hearts' desire fills with these things leaving less room for God. Cleanse, empty, extinguish, and make space in your heart and soul for God's love.

❦ Deepen your prayer life. Grow spiritually. Have you read the Bible? I thought about this years ago and, having not read the Bible myself, I shuddered at my ingratitude for the Word of God. I wondered how hurt Jesus must be that so many children of God have not taken the time to read the Word of God. I slowly began to read the Scriptures, maybe fifteen minutes at night before going to bed (if I remembered to do it).

Thankfully, there are so many ways to read the Bible. Please don't feel overwhelmed by the size of it; you don't need to read it in one sitting or a year! Read ten minutes a day or read a couple of chapters a day. Most of the chapters are short. Start with the Gospels since the Good News of Jesus will be the most familiar. The Bible is a fascinating collection of books. Decide to read a book a month. As you read the Old Testament, you will hear the words of the prophets that Jesus, the Messiah, fulfilled in the New Testament. Use a study bible because, if you are like me, you will value the corresponding commentary that explains and gives historical context to the biblical text. There are narrated audio versions, videos, and audiobooks of the Bible. If you are a Catholic Christian, become a dedicated reader of the daily Mass readings (including the daily Psalms). In three years, you will have read the entire Bible.

❦ Love your enemies. Why? Because God loves us, every one of us, unconditionally. Just because you may have been offended or hurt by someone doesn't lessen God's love for that person. Forgive. Accept apologies gracefully. And if the apology does not come, forgive anyway. Don't hold onto grudges. Pray for your enemies, you'll feel better about yourself, and it will engulf your soul in love and peace. Love your enemies because Jesus said so in His Sermon on the Mount:

> But I say to you, love your enemies, and pray for those who persecute you, that you may be children of your heavenly Father, for he makes his sun rise on the bad and the good, and causes rain to fall on the just and unjust.
> —Matthew 5:44–45

The well-being of the soul isn't only about temptation and sin. There are so many things of a positive nature we can do in our daily lives to care for our souls, many of which have already been discussed in this book. I do find the following to be thought-provoking messages, good reminders, and tenderness for the soul.

Live a life of gratitude.
Be gentle with yourself.
Give yourself grace when you stumble or make mistakes.
Speak out against injustice.
Receive compliments graciously. Compliment others.
Admit and apologize for any wrongdoings—it has a freeing effect.
Be patient with yourself and others.
Be temperate in food and drink.
Regularly reflect on your acts of goodness and kindness, thanking God for each opportunity.
Give God all praise and glory. Do everything in Jesus' name.

> A little holiness and great health of body does more in the care of souls than great holiness and little health.
> —Ignatius of Loyola, *Epistolae S. Ignatii*

Taking care of our mind, body, and soul is necessary for loving ourselves. Only when we are in a healthy place, have begun the healing process, or have accepted a condition as

God's will that we can truly "love your neighbor as yourself" as Jesus expects.

To love one another as God loves us, we must love ourselves as God loves us.

With an understanding of the importance of loving and caring for ourselves as we set out to play our part in the Body of Christ, you may also realize that this pertains not only to you but to every member of this Body. When we are better able to "love your neighbor as yourself," we will be much better aligned, more willing, and more open to collaborating with and helping each other keep the light and face of Jesus Christ alive in the world. In the next chapter, we will explore what it might look like to do this work—In Communion.

14
IN COMMUNION

> Then the apostles and presbyters, in agreement with the whole church, decided to choose representatives and to send them to Antioch with Paul and Barnabas. The ones chosen were Judas, who was called Barsabbas, and Silas, leaders among the brothers.
>
> —Acts of the Apostles 15:22

> All baptized Christians have a unique and vital part to play in building up the Body of Christ. When one fails to fulfill their role, the Church cannot attain its ultimate promise.
>
> —Marty Mitchell

On October 16, 1978, Karol Wojtyla became the first pope from a communist country, choosing the name John Paul II. The new pope lived under communist rule in his homeland of Poland. He was an outspoken opponent of the communist government ideology of the Soviet Union and many Eastern European countries. He decried the forced atheism and the lack of religious freedom that came along with totalitarian control.

THE CAPILLARIES OF CHRIST

In June of 1979, during the first year of his papacy, John Paul II made a historic visit to Poland. Although the country was officially atheist, there were still millions of followers of Christianity, a most of whom were Roman Catholic.

The Pope celebrated an outdoor Mass within hours of arriving on June 2 and estimates suggested over a million Polish pilgrims converged on the site to participate. I can only imagine the crowd was ecstatic that one of their own, now Pope John Paul II, was not only standing on Polish soil, but he was also celebrating Mass in the shadow of the communist officials in Warsaw, the capital of his motherland.

During his sermon, The Pope told the people:

> For man cannot be fully understood without Christ. Or rather, man is incapable of understanding himself fully without Christ. He cannot understand who he is, nor what his true dignity is, nor what his vocation is, nor what his final end is. He cannot understand any of this without Christ.
>
> Therefore Christ cannot be kept out of the history of man in any part of the globe, at any longitude or latitude of geography. The exclusion of Christ from the history of man is an act against man…And the history of each person unfolds in Jesus Christ.

In the middle of the homily, the faithful in attendance broke out in a spontaneous song and began to chant, "We Want God. We Want God." It lasted nearly 15 minutes.

Pope John Paul II ended his words with this prayer: "And I cry—I who am a Son of the land of Poland and who am also Pope John Paul II—I cry from all the depths of this Millennium; I cry on the vigil of Pentecost: Let your Spirit descend. Let your Spirit descend. And renew the face of the earth, the face of this land. Amen."[1]

The words of The Pope and the reaction of the faithful, working in communion in what was tantamount to a peaceful revolution, became the event that triggered the Solidarity movement in Poland and, ultimately, the fall of communism in Eastern Europe just ten years later.

When Christians work together, amazing things happen. Christianity rose into the decade of the 1980s to usher in a triumphant shift in the political, social, and economic landscape in that part of the world. Citizens were granted religious freedom. People could soon vote for representative leaders and policies in competitive and free elections. Maps were forever changed. Physical walls and social barriers were torn down. Just as He did at Pentecost to give the Church of Christ a new and everlasting life, God in the Holy Spirit descended into the hearts of the world to "renew the face of the earth, the face of this land."

The Latin root of the word communion is *communionem* meaning "fellowship, mutual participation, sharing" (vocabulary.com). The apostle Paul and the first disciples lived and acted in communion as they spread the Good News of the Gospel and baptized the earliest Christians, filling them with the Holy Spirit (Acts 19:6) and giving the Church a strong foundation.

Why in communion? For a lot of reasons, I suppose. They encouraged each other (2 Cor. 1:3–7), "proclaimed the word of God" (Acts 13:5), and traveled together (Acts 20:4–6), all by Jesus' design when He sent His disciples in pairs to be His witnesses.

They did it to support and to pray for each other and their mission. Each disciple may have had strengths and weaknesses that complimented the other partner in preaching the Word of God. Their personalities may have differed such that their unique style and approach would appeal to the various groups with whom they would interact. It's possible Jesus sent a senior disciple with one who hadn't followed Him for as long and who may not have had as much confidence or understanding of all that Jesus had been teaching. Maybe being able to collaborate with a partner on this mission deepened friendship and unity, offered protection, gave them credibility, fostered an exchange of ideas, and bred encouragement.

For these reasons and for the spirit of cooperation, Christians today should not only play their unique part in the Body of Christ but also be willing to work with others when opportunities arise to support and magnify each other's contribution in drawing people closer to Christ. Fulton Sheen wrote, "What would happen to our human bodies if our hands and feet and lips refused to co-operate with the other parts of our bodies? Something analogously sad and tragic happens to the Mystical Body when some of its members fail."[2]

You have likely worked with a group of people pursuing a common cause, whether on a project at school or work, supporting a ministry at church, or with friends planning and contributing to a surprise party or other social event. Some in the group will usually take the lead, while others pitch in where they can. Inevitably, there are always people who don't carry their weight to the group's detriment.

So it is in the Body of Christ. Every Christian is a vital member of this Body. Through collaboration with others, we are doing the work of Jesus, all working in communion to build up the Church and to keep the light and face of

Jesus Christ alive in the world. Remember, our gifts bear fruit when done out of love and in Jesus' name, be it simple and small, more skillful or talented, or in cooperation with another person or with many more on a larger scale.

> "It is your task and mine to assist all those who cross our paths to fulfill their destiny. Serving others in this way will also allow us to fulfill our own destiny. This is one of the brilliant and beautiful ways that God has tied us all together."[3]
> —Matthew Kelly, *Rediscover Catholicism*

It is important here to mention two essential groups within the Body of Christ—Christian youth and families. The Second Vatican Council (1962–1965) and the associated documents offer rich expressions about these subjects. I would do them and these two groups injustice if I attempted to paraphrase it in any way.

Significantly, though, I want to point out that non-Catholic Christian leaders (+/- 75) were also involved in this Council. According to Vatican II–Voice of The Church, "A number of senior members of other Christian denominations were invited to the Council as observers and were not infrequently valuable in private discussions."[4] The Council is credited with a new movement toward Christian unity.[5]

The quotes that follow from the "Decree on the Apostolate of the Laity–*Apostolicam Actuositatem*"[6] were written in the early 1960s yet are just as relevant today. (This document indicates all the activity of the Body of Christ directed to the attainment of the purposes of the Church is called the apostolate.) I love how the youth and their role within their circle of friends are acknowledged and described:

> Young persons exert very important influence in modern society.... Their heightened influence in society demands of them a proportionate apostolic activity, but their natural qualities also fit them for this activity. As they become more conscious of their own personalities, they are impelled by a zest for life and a ready eagerness to assume their own responsibility, and they yearn to play their part in social and cultural life. If this zeal is imbued with the spirit of Christ and is inspired by obedience and love for the Church, it can be expected to be very fruitful. They should become the first to carry on the apostolate directly to other young persons, concentrating their apostolic efforts within their own circle, according to the needs of the social environment in which they live.[7]

Our youth (commonly described as preteens to early twenties) have a vital role in the Body of Christ. Who would be better to meet other adolescents where they are than one of their own who lives a passionate life inspired by the Holy Spirit and love for the Lord? As a group, young people have a zest for being social. They are well situated to work in communion with friends of shared Christian values to deepen their faith, love their neighbor, and be a shining light for others navigating through this formative stage of life. Awareness of and compassion for less fortunate people tends to blossom in these years.

On social media, our youth can be a good Christian example for others by being positive and modest and interacting with a loving heart—in contrast to taking the negative, immodest, or hate-filled road down which so many travel.

Let's also know that our youth have excellent potential, standing side-by-side with Christians of all ages, filled with the same Holy Spirit, to positively influence the effort toward building the Body of Christ. The energy, eagerness, optimism, brightness, and love that flow from them are attractive and magnetic. When working in communion with the wisdom and direction of those more experienced in life, it can be a powerful collaboration that Jesus can use to continue building His kingdom on Earth.

The spiritual zeal of our youth is often nurtured through the love that is shared within families. The family is the domestic church (*Lumen Gentium* #11) because this is where children are first introduced to the One True God, the Holy Trinity, the sacred Scriptures, prayer, attending church, the sacraments, and Christian traditions and values. The family is a community that grows together in the Christian faith.

> This mission—to be the first and vital cell of society–the family has received from God. It will fulfill this mission if it appears as the domestic sanctuary of the Church by reason of the mutual affection of its members and the prayer that they offer to God in common, if the whole family makes itself a part of the liturgical worship of the Church, and if it provides active hospitality and promotes justice and other good works for the service of all the brethren in need.[8]

Promoting justice and other good works for the service of those in need stems from Jesus, the Vine, in His instructions to love one another as He loves us, to love your neighbor as yourself, and to love the least of His (and our) brothers and sisters.

As children, specific experiences and traditions provided by our parents leave an impression, shape who we become, and create the memories we want our children to experience.

When I was a youngster, I remember my family of seven gathering around the television each year on Labor Day weekend to watch the Jerry Lewis MDA Telethon benefiting the Muscular Dystrophy Association. The stories and lives of those affected by this disease were touching and inspirational, if not heartbreaking. We watched the on-camera volunteers monitoring the phones and taking calls while the donation board clicked higher toward the lofty monetary goal. At preteen ages and younger, my siblings and I couldn't wait to make a call to donate some of the little we had in our piggy banks or savings accounts.

Being able to be part of a global effort to raise money for this association and these kids gave our family a sense of coming together for a greater cause working in communion with each other and with all those who participated in the fund-raising campaign. While I didn't realize it then, one of the lessons our parents provided for us in those telethons was that true charity is giving out of our poverty, not our surplus (Mark 12:41-44).

Many family traditions revolve around the sights, sounds, and smells of attending church, worshiping, and enjoying personal relationships with other families and friends built on common faith and shared morals and values. Staying after to enjoy donuts, coffee, and conversation or attending dinners in the church hall foster friendships, unity, and socializing around the community. Volunteering together as a family and with other Christians in community outreach programs instills a shared responsibility to provide for those in need.

In the home, sharing meals and saying grace together when our busy schedules allow, laughing together, showing a genuine interest in each other's activities, and praying together regularly all build that special bond found only in families. In younger families, game nights and playing with or hanging out with our siblings create great fun and laughter. Still, it teaches sharing, sportsmanship, social skills, and sometimes even conflict resolution. It is here that our youth begin to blossom into their unique personalities and may even be a source of training for that budding God-given talent entrusted to them to use to glorify God in the Body of Christ.

> The sun looks down on nothing half so good as a household laughing together over a meal.
> —C.S. Lewis, *The Weight of Glory* (1949, 161)

As I noted, every Christian has a vitally collaborative part to play in the Body of Christ. When one suffers, we all suffer. When one is honored, we all share in that joy (1 Cor. 12:26). We must "bear one another's burdens" (Gal. 6:2). Paul also writes about the need for each part of the Body to function properly for the sake of the growth of the Body and building itself up in love (Eph. 4:16).

The writings of the Vatican II Decree referenced above also explicitly describe the responsibility we have to the Body of Christ and each other:

> No part of the structure of a living body is merely passive but has a share in the functions as well as the life of the body: so, too, the body of Christ, which is the Church.... the member who fails to make his proper contribution to

the development of the Church must be said to be useful neither to the Church nor to himself.[9]

Wow! Are they talking about me? Have I failed so badly that I am useless to the Church and myself? It certainly is a thought-provoking admonishment! To be sure, this warning is not issued in vain. It is up to each of us to honestly assess our contribution and to make positive changes where necessary.

However, before we get too worked up about this, most of you reading this book have likely contributed far more than you know. Keep in mind The Little Way of St. Thérèse of Lisieux. You are playing your part by doing anything with love and in the name of Jesus, no matter how insignificant you think it is. If you carry and express any of the fruits of the Holy Spirit with you wherever you are, He's working through you to play your part. For example, if you offer a smile to a stranger with love and kindness in your heart, you are bearing witness to Christ.

Think of all the times in the past when you acted in a Christ-like manner. Can we always do more? Absolutely. Your interest in reading this book indicates your desire and inclination to do more. It also suggests the Holy Spirit is leading you to become more aware of the many possibilities to play your unique part on your own and with others. He's also likely nudging you to take your next best step toward increasing your contribution, helping others do the same, and "…to encourage one another to Christian love and activity" (NABRE notes to Heb. 10:19–39, v. 24).

This quote from St. Teresa of Calcutta is a terrific reminder to seek ways to partner with others as we work to draw people closer to God through the Body of Christ.

I can do things you cannot, you can do things I cannot, together we can do great things.

And this from Msgr. Owen Campion of the Diocese of Fort Wayne – South Bend:

> The community of believers is not a happenstance of people standing side by side. In the Spirit they share one source of life. Thus, Christians act in communion—ideally.[10]

Sometimes it takes more clarified intention to develop the awareness needed to see the possibilities and the doors that open for us. It often takes trust and confidence in the Lord to take steps that stretch us or that may take us into unfamiliar experiences. We will cover this more in Part 5. But first, in Chapter 15, let's discover more about the Holy Spirit and His constant companionship, communication, and desire to collaborate with us to realize we are—Never Alone.

15
NEVER ALONE

> And I will ask the Father, and he will give you another
> Advocate to be with you always, the Spirit of truth, which the
> world cannot accept, because it neither sees nor knows it. But
> you know it, because it remains with you, and will be in you.
> —John 14:16-17

> Holy Spirit, I am thirsting for you.
> Let your life well up within me.
> —The Word Among Us

> The living cell in the healthy human body is never alone;
> it is perpetually infused with life-giving blood.

Jesus Christ is Emmanuel. What a beautiful name first foretold by the Holy Spirit through the prophet Isaiah (Isa. 7:14) more than 700 years before the birth of Jesus. The angel repeated it in a dream to explain to Joseph why he shouldn't divorce Mary, who became pregnant without having relations with her betrothed (a legal commitment to marry):

> All this took place to fulfill what the Lord had said through the prophet: "Behold, the virgin shall be with child and bear a son, and shall name him Emmanuel," which means "God is with us.
> —Matthew 1:22–23

Of course, as Christians, we know the rest of the annunciation (announcement) story told in Luke 1:26–38 that Jesus, the Son of God, was conceived by the Holy Spirit in the womb of the virgin Mary. Born in Bethlehem on that first Christmas, Jesus, the Christ, anointed by the Holy Spirit, is God incarnate and the image of the invisible God (Col. 1:15).

Emmanuel. God is with us. The name doesn't mean God is with us for a minute or a few years. It doesn't mean He would only be with us while Jesus walked on this earth. In the final line of Matthew's Gospel, Jesus, the Word of God made flesh, also proclaimed this Emmanuel before ascending to the Father when he said:

> And, behold, I am with you always, until the end of the age.
> —Matthew 28:20

God is with us always, and He is with us infinitely. He is with us in Holy Communion, the Sacred Scriptures, the sacraments, prayer, the Church, and the Body of Christ. He is with us in His Spirit, who reveals all these things to the faithful. Not only is He with us, but the Spirit of God also dwells in us (1 Cor. 3:16; John 14:17).

The Spirit of God, the Father, is the Spirit of Christ (Rom. 8:9), the Holy Spirit who proceeds from the Father and the Son. God is with us.

When the Advocate comes whom I will send you from the Father, the Spirit of truth that proceeds from the Father, he will testify to me.

—John 15:26

The One whom the Father has sent into our hearts, the Spirit of his Son, is truly God. Consubstantial with the Father and the Son, the Spirit is inseparable from them, in both the inner life of the Trinity and his gift of love for the world (CCC 689).

Undeniably, we are never alone.

The Holy Spirit is our constant companion in us and all around us at the same time. He is our friend, guiding and leading us in our thoughts, actions, words, and deeds.

To collaborate in this holy and divine friendship, to be His dear friend, and to live our Best Blessed Life™, it is essential for us to be present with Him, to recognize how He is working in us and what He may be revealing to us, and to listen and look for Him. When we do these things well, we will grow in our intimacy with Jesus, our hearts will overflow with God's peace, love, and joy, and we will readily embrace the part we are to play in the Body of Christ. He will move us to take Christ-centered steps in the present moment, aligned with the will of God.

BE PRESENT WITH HIM

> The past does not belong to me; the future is not mine; with all my soul I try to make use of the present moment.
> —St. Faustina, *Diary of Saint Maria Faustina Kowalska*

Live in the present moment. The present moment is where we will find and receive guidance from Jesus in the Holy Spirit. We spend so much of our time and thoughts concerned with or happily remembering what happened yesterday or anticipating what may happen tomorrow. It's so interesting.

The past has come and gone; we cannot change a bit of it. Happy memories may comfort the mind and soul, and times of emotional and spiritual growth and breakthroughs are pleasing to look back on and celebrate. The mistakes from which we can learn may grate on our hearts, however. The Holy Spirit is no longer there, though. He dwells in us right now.

The future has yet to arrive. How we imagine it, good and joyful, difficult and challenging, mundane or exciting, will never materialize exactly how we expect, and it may never arrive! The Holy Spirit doesn't live in the future, either. Yes, in God's providence, He is all-knowing from the beginning to the end of time. However, He lives in our hearts and longs for us to abide in His love (John 15:4–5). Where do we find it? In the present moment, the here and now.

> As to the past, let us entrust it to God's mercy, the future to divine providence. Our task is to live holy in the present moment.[1]
> —St. Gianna Molla

I must admit living in the present is a challenging endeavor. We live in an age of never-ending distraction. Turning off our distractions, concerns, memories, to-dos, anxieties, pressing matters, and worries is not easy. Yet, to live in the present moment with Jesus in the Holy Spirit, we must train our minds and hearts to do just that.

Why? Because God speaks in whispers (1 Kings 19:11–13). He waits for us in silence and solitude. When our minds and hearts are full of clutter, we can't turn our focus to His presence in our souls, His presence all around us, His presence before us, and His presence helping us.

If we aren't living with Him in the present moment, we may not hear Him knocking at the door of our hearts and inviting us to His heavenly banquet. If we aren't with Him in the present, we may not hear His voice and open that door (Rev. 3:20).

Here are some tips on living in the present moment with God:

Lift your mind and heart to Him in prayer. As you go about your day, speak the breath prayers or find a quiet place to enter a lengthier period of prayer.

Always be listening for Him in the Holy Spirit, and recognize when He is encouraging you to act in that moment.

Ask the Holy Spirit to remind you that He is with you always.

Seek His wisdom in the seconds before you enter a conversation or interact with someone else. Let Him counsel you on what to say, what not to say, and when to listen.

Let Him guide all your actions, interactions, reactions, and inaction.

Spend time reading, listening to, and watching faith-based content from trusted Christian sources. Spend time in the Word of God (especially soon after a new day begins).

Offer everything you do, no matter how insignificant you may think it is, be offered in Jesus' name.

What is the present moment? To answer this, I turn to my mother's side of the family. Mom's father had six first cousins from the same Irish Catholic family—three boys and three girls.[2] Around 1930, each chose to commit their lives to the Lord, with the boys entering the seminary and ordained as priests and the girls entering the convent and making their vows as nuns. All six lived a monastic life.

Father Marion Walsh O.S.B. was the cousin and priest with whom my mother was closest. Mom told me Fr. Marion once told her:

> This is the most precious moment, this one right now. This one. Not the one that came before. Not the one that will come next. This one, this moment is the most precious moment.

Recognize How He is Working in Us and What He is Revealing

What a blessing it is to have received the **anointing** of the Holy Spirit at baptism and to have Him actively **dwelling** in us and all around us in these ways:

teaching and **interpreting** the scriptures and the spiritual truths received from God that we then share with others (1 Cor. 2:13)[3] and **reminding** us of all that Jesus has told us (John 14:26).

guiding us to all truth, **speaking** only what He hears from the Father through Jesus, and **declaring** and **telling** us what is to come (John 16:13–15).

leading, helping, and strengthening us (Rom. 8:14, 26).

encouraging (NABRE) **and comforting** (RSV-CE) us (2 Cor. 1:1–7).

interceding in prayer "with inexpressible groanings" for those who "according to God's will" are called "holy ones" (Rom. 8:26–27).

convicting and convincing the world concerning sin (John 16:8).

revealing who Jesus Christ is and the proper way to speak of Him (1 Cor. 12:3).

sanctifying us–being made holy (2 Thess. 2:13; Rom. 1:4; 15:16; 1 Peter 1:2).

The Holy Spirit is here for us, actively engaging with us so that, by our free will, we may live life in the Spirit, not in the flesh (Gal. 5:16; Rom. 8:1-13). He is our friend and our constant companion. He is pulling for us and paving the way to bear good fruit in the Body of Christ.

When the Spirit encounters in us the response of faith which he has aroused in us, he brings about genuine cooperation.

—CCC 1091

Spend time with Him in prayer, asking Him to do these things for you, your family, and all Christians. Contemplate these action words and recognize when and how the Spirit has revealed these workings to you in the past and present and will do so again in the future. He is doing this for you; yes, for YOU! Talk with Him, thank Him, love Him.

Listen and Look for Him

We all have that internal narrative, that voice in our head to which we tend to listen more than anyone or anything else. Also called our conscience, it is that quiet yet resounding whisper that directs our thoughts even in the loudest of surroundings. We hardly miss what our conscience is saying to us despite all the distractions, worries, and anxieties that keep us from living in the present moment with God. How interesting, and how can this be?

Merriam-Webster defines conscience as a state of awareness or a sense that one's actions or intentions are either morally right or wrong, along with the feeling of obligation to do the right thing.

Moral conscience forms the perception and knowledge of right from wrong. For a theological and more scholarly definition of the relationship between moral conscience (law) and God, the documents of Vatican II[4] (*GS* sec. 16) tell us:

Deep within his conscience man discovers a law which he has not laid upon himself but which he must obey. Its voice, ever calling him to love and to do what is good and to avoid evil, sounds in his heart at the right moment. . . . For man has in his heart a law inscribed by God. . . . His conscience is man's most secret core and his sanctuary. There he is alone with God whose voice echoes in his depths.

Therein lies the answer to the question I posed above. How can we hear our conscience over everything else and find it so difficult to live with God in the present moment? Because it is God who inscribes this moral law on our hearts, and when we spend time listening in this most secret core and sanctuary, we can hear the voice of God. We do find ourselves in His presence. "When he listens to his conscience, the prudent man can hear God speaking" (CCC 1777).

To develop a well-formed conscience, the Word of God lights our path (Ps. 119:105), and we get assistance from the gifts of the Holy Spirit and guidance to all truth through the Holy Spirit (CCC 1785). In his letter to the Romans, Paul wrote:

> I speak the truth in Christ, I do not lie; my conscience joins with the holy Spirit in bearing me witness.
> —Romans 9:1

Listen for Him. When I hear Jesus speaking through the Holy Spirit, it is often in the same realm where I hear my conscience. Sometimes I find it difficult to tell the two apart, and others, when I know with certainty what I just heard was the Holy Spirit. It may not be "as loud as a trumpet" as when the apostle John heard the voice of Christ in his first vision in Revelation 1:10. But He makes Himself heard in a distinguishable voice that I immediately recognize.

I often react with, "whoa, THAT was the Holy Spirit," and I've come to know I better listen to Him and respond. Do you know how sometimes a thought suddenly comes to mind? If it's a morally good thought that is "of God", it is probably the Holy Spirit putting that thought in your mind and on your heart.

An example could be when we feel moved to pray for someone or to text or call another with a message of hope and support. Or maybe you ask God for healing for yourself or someone in your family and hear an internal voice telling you to get down on your knees. It's probably a good idea to get down on your knees!

Your experiences with the Holy Spirit might be similar, or they may be quite different.

I also go through dry spells when I don't hear Him at all, not because He isn't communicating with me but because I am just not listening as I should, or perhaps I've headed down a sinful path.

I've found the Holy Spirit wise, clever, and creative, revealing Himself in many forms. And why not? After all, He showed up in numerous ways throughout the Bible, accompanied by a dove, fire, a gentle breeze, a noise like a strong driving wind, breath, a whisper, water, a cloud, light, and thunder.

Listen and look for Him from the heart. Listen with the ear of our hearts and see with the eyes of our hearts (Eph. 1:18) because it is in our hearts where the Spirit of the God of love, who is the Spirit of Christ, resides. When we listen and look from our heart, we will notice God's radiant presence all around us and see how he is working with and among us. We will recognize the opportunities He provides us to grow in our intimacy with Him and play our part in the Body of Christ. We will be "enlightened, that you may know what is the hope that belongs to his call, what are the riches of glory in his inheritance among the holy ones" (v. 18). We will know the inheritance that Jesus secured for us by dying on the cross and rising from the dead.

> So then the Lord Jesus, after he spoke to them, was taken up into heaven and took his seat at the right hand of God. But they went forth and preached everywhere, while the Lord worked with them and confirmed the word through accompanying signs.
> —Mark 16:19–20

Where else can we find the Holy Spirit? The signs of His presence may not be as apparent as when Mark wrote about the apostles driving out demons or speaking new languages (Mark 16:17). The signs of the workings of the invisible Spirit twenty centuries later tend to be more subtle. Yet, they will be evident if we look for and are open to them.

He meets us right where we are. Think about how this may have or could manifest in your life.

- He speaks to us through scripture when a verse jumps out when we need it for consolation, hope, confirmation, or encouragement. Have you ever had this experience reading scripture where it feels like He is speaking directly to you? It's because He is!
- It is incredible how often a daily devotional we read addresses what we are going through or anticipating at that time. One time? That's probably coincidental. Regularly? That must be divine.

- He speaks through a friend who, unbeknownst to this person, says or does something that answers our prayer.
- We testify in church or to some friends that Jesus is our Savior. The apostle Paul tells us no one can say this on their own; it comes from the Holy Spirit (1 Cor.12:3).
- Out of the blue, a close colleague brings a spiritual book we've heard about and wanted to get. Undoubtedly, the Holy Spirit led that person to do this.
- We notice something on a billboard or bumper sticker that speaks to us in that moment.
- We hear a voice in our head (or heart) that gives us the nudge to clear the snow off the vehicle of an older or unable neighbor.
- We get an uplifting card from a friend or sibling at a time when our spirits need a boost.
- We receive a positive affirmation that we are on the right path. Perhaps it's a promotion at work, a new opportunity (open door) that advances our efforts, a new relationship, or a small sign that we're doing the right thing at a time when we are beginning to question ourselves.
- In contemplative prayer, we hear the voice of Jesus through the Holy Spirit.
- Invited by God, when we pray, it is the Holy Spirit, "the master of prayer" (CCC 741), who prays with and for us "for we do not know how to pray as we ought…" (Rom. 8:26). He guides us toward conforming what we ask for in prayer to the will of the Father, in Jesus' name.
- After hemming and hawing about running out to the store, we finally do just in time to hear something on

the car radio that reminds us how important we are in God's eyes, reinforces how much we should trust Him, and makes us feel His loving presence in our soul.
- It is the Holy Spirit who animates and preserves all life (CCC 703). Having a hand in creation, here specifically in the Garden of Eden (Gen. 2:4–15), He surrounds us in nature. His presence can be felt in a cool gentle breeze on a warm summer day, the melody of the bird that breaks the silence of the night, the rays of sunlight that fan out from behind the clouds, the roar of the invisible wind on a stormy day, the beautiful rising and setting of the sun.

> When they heard the sound of the Lord God walking about in the garden at the breezy time of the day, the man and his wife hid themselves.
> —Genesis 3:8

That's the Holy Spirit! Invite Him daily to be awakened in you and to ignite His fire within you. Notice Him. Greet Him. Love Him. Sit in silence with Him. Collaborate with Him. Listen for His promptings to act in the moment, to use your gifts and talents, and to play your part in the Body of Christ.

In these excerpts from his classic *The Mystical Body of Christ* (first published in 1935), Fulton Sheen expressed beautifully just how close the Trinitarian God is to us even to this day and until the end of time.

> Thanks to His invisible Spirit which He sends into His Mystical Body, Christ is living now on earth just as really and truly as He was living in Galilee nineteen centuries ago. In a certain sense He is closer to us now than then,

for His very Body made him external to us, but thanks to His Spirit, He can live in us as the very Soul of our souls, the very Spirit of our spirit, the Truth of our minds, the Love of our hearts, and the Desire of our wills…

The joys that come from human friendships, even the noblest, are but shadows and reflections of the joy of a soul possessed of the Spirit of Christ. Elevate human happiness which comes from union with the one loved to the most extreme point the heart can endure, and even that is but a spark compared to the flame of the Spirit of Christ burning in a soul that loves Him" (Sheen 2015, 183–184).

We are never alone.

It's time to put what we've been able to discern into action wherever we are and however we can in our current stage in life and in our own unique way based the person God has blessed us to be. We will be inspired to become ever so aware of the world around us, to live with intention each day, and to accept the call to holiness, as we are sent forth in Part 5—Commission.

PART 5

Commission

Go, therefore, and make disciples of all nations, baptizing them in the name of the Father, and of the Son, and of the holy Spirit, teaching them to observe all that I have commanded you.
—Matthew 28:19–20

Just as the heart sends forth the blood and individual blood cells to carry oxygen and other nutrients to the extremities of the human body, the Holy Spirit sends forth the Church and individual Christians in the Body of Christ to carry the light and face of Jesus to the corners of the world.
—Marty Mitchell

16
BE ALIVE!

I will instruct you and teach you the way you should go;
I will counsel you with my eye upon you.
—Psalm 32:8 (RSV-CE)

Every act of compassion and service, every breath of prayer or of healing, is an emphatic statement that Jesus is alive and in our midst. May we live what we believe!
—Sr. Chris Koellhoffer, I.H.M, *Living Faith*, November 23, 2019

Can you imagine yourself in ten years if, instead of avoiding the things you know you should do, you actually did them every single day? That's powerful.
—Jordan Peterson (@JBPetersonQuote, Twitter, Feb 24, 2019)

Despite age and state of life, you and I, and all baptized Christians worldwide, have a vital function to perform and a unique part to play in keeping the one Body of Christ healthy, growing, vigorous, and alive.

We do this by reflecting the visible light of Jesus from within ourselves, recognizing Him in others, and sharing the love of God with one another in our unique and creative way. We are equipped for this because of the unceasing presence of the Holy Spirit in our hearts and souls and the Body of Christ.

What a privilege it is to be a member of the Body of Christ! Not because we obtain special rights or advantages but in a humble sense; with it comes great responsibility to embrace and cherish.

> The responsibility to extend the Mystical Body of Christ falls upon each of its members. Any member who refuses it is guilty of a breach of trust. The privilege of being a cell in the Mystical Body is the privilege of stewardship and service and propagation.[1]
> —Fulton Sheen

Let's be alive and energized in our faith and keenly aware of the opportunities presented to us from above to love one another as Jesus loves us throughout our day-to-day lives. With this as our intention in every waking moment, we can remain attached to the Vine and be ready to bear good fruit when called upon. We will also tend to be more aware of temptations as they arise and better able to ignore them, so our connection to the Vine does not weaken.

Intention and awareness, they go together. When put into action, we walk on the path of love and we are filled with peace and joy. The more we do it, the more we want to do it. Let's take a closer look at living with intention and awareness in the Body of Christ for the greater glory of God.

Living with intention doesn't need to require a lot of effort. It doesn't. All it requires is a firm commitment to live with a purpose and to do what it takes to make it happen. Think about the mindless effort we make every day and how this allows us to accomplish greater goals.

- One of the first things we do every day, half asleep, is to brush our teeth with the intention of keeping them and our gums healthy and our breath clean and fresh.
- We eat our meals with the intention of satisfying our hunger and giving our bodies the nutrients and energy needed to stay strong and perform our daily duties.
- Many of us travel to work intending to use our skills to earn a fair wage that will allow us to pay our bills and support ourselves or our families.

You get the point. Now, these examples are all "of the world" where we have some control over the outcome.

To live with the intention of playing our part in the Body of Christ requires seeking the will of God and being responsive to the promptings of the Holy Spirit. The daily purpose we need to acquire is to awaken each day committed to being aware of what we can do today to share God's love with others with what He has given us (time, talent, and treasure) and to be willing to do it with compassion in the present moment as the Holy Spirit guides us.

Because divinity is at the Head and Soul of the Body of Christ, the life and flow of this Body are mysteriously fluid and unannounced. Indeed, that to which we are called to respond can be more spontaneous than what seems to be the structure and relative predictability in our worldly lives (brushing our teeth, for example).

You may have had experiences where you crossed paths with someone, heard something from someone that spoke to you, or saw something happen that led you to think or exclaim with surprise, "That was a God-thing!"

This quote from St. Augustine paints the picture of paying attention and being aware:

> Since you cannot do good to all, you are to pay special attention to those who, by the accidents of time, or place, or circumstances, are brought into closer connection with you.

Humanity and the supernatural coexist in the Body of Christ. Jesus and the Holy Spirit put it on our hearts to live with the purpose of playing our divinely prescribed part in the here and now. In our humanity, it is our free will that resists and often gets in the way.

When we wake up every morning and dedicate our attention, awareness, and intention toward seeking the path of love with all whom we encounter, by the grace of God, our free will can begin to align with His will. We will start to notice how often He provides for us to play our part in the Body of Christ. Remember, it could be something as simple as a smile or a helping hand. Or it may be something more involved. Whatever it is, just be open to seeing it and willing to do it. If it is God's will, He will provide everything needed to accomplish it.

Jesus desires a personal and intimate relationship with all humanity. Sadly, so many in the world decline this invitation to be alive in Christ, welcome Him into their hearts, and receive Him as their savior. He is so very loving, merciful, and patient, and He awaits the slightest inkling, motion, or thought directed toward Him to pour His Spirit into the tiniest crack in a hardened heart.

We, the baptized and faithful believers in the Body of Christ, want nothing more than to welcome and embrace these hearts and to walk with them as brothers and sisters in the kingdom of God.

God wants nothing less than for the entire human race to be saved (1 Tim. 2:3–6). He's watching to see how well we attract others to Him by how we live, love, and exemplify Jesus Christ. All this takes place during our everyday living. Once we do, the Holy Spirit will move in to do the rest.

This personal relationship with the Holy Trinity is available for all Christians to enjoy, but it can't be private. On the contrary, it must be shared and displayed for all to see! We experience our faith and relationship with God in similar and different ways. That's precisely why it must be shared so our hearts and minds will be open to and aware of the possibilities.

How I live with the intention of playing my part in the Body of Christ may differ from what works best for you. My experience in this may be helpful for others, and hearing what works best for others can open my eyes to new ways of living with intention and playing my part. (This interaction and sharing our faith and experiences with Jesus in the Holy Spirit is one of the benefits of joining a community of like-hearted souls, whether in your school, your church, or in a group online. Doing so may increase our desire to live with intention.)

As I get out of bed in the morning, the first thing I always try to do is to tell Jesus I love Him and thank Him for the new day. I then think about living with intention and awareness—not with any specificity, but that I am committed to this. When this is one of my first thoughts, it stays in the front of my mind throughout the day.

When I started living with this intention, I became much more aware of the Holy Spirit and how He led and guided me. Over time, as situations developed, I could anticipate that I might be hearing from Him. It typically starts with my visual acknowledgment (awareness) as an opportunity presents itself. I may not immediately feel inclined to do anything until I hear His soft words, or He pulls at my heartstrings to do something.

Once this happens, there is no turning back; I want to step forward in trust. I don't question it. I realize He presented me with this opportunity for a reason. The grace of God brought together the other person(s) and me. I know it, and I feel the push to act with love. With God, I believe there are no coincidences.

It becomes a mindset, with my heart set on doing the will of God or, at least, what I perceive to be His will. When I leave my home, I make a point of being aware of what is happening around me. Whom can I help? How can I help? How might I use my God-given traits to show others the face of Jesus, to be someone's servant, or to brighten their day?

> Do you want to do something beautiful for God? There is a person who needs you. This is your chance.[2]
> —St. Teresa of Calcutta

One morning, I was driving on a three-lane highway to an appointment. On a side road on my right, I noticed there was a disheveled man pushing an overflowing shopping cart. He was headed in the opposite direction than I was going. It was an unusual place to find a homeless person because it wasn't near any town center. Besides, the side road was perpendicular to several neighborhood entrances.

My heart felt for this guy as the Holy Spirit began to work in me. I had about a quarter of a mile to listen for what He was saying. "You're plenty early for this appointment. You have time and space to switch lanes safely to get off at the next exit. From there, you'll be able to circle back to that side road to help him and then get back on your way."

As I'm listening and considering these same things, all in a split second, I'm already putting them into motion. There was no apprehension, only peace that this was what I was supposed to do and a feeling of heartache for this man.

As I approached from behind, I could see him talking with himself, or perhaps, to a voice he could hear in his head. Thinking back on it, it could have been the Holy Spirit keeping him company. I drove by him to the next neighborhood entrance and turned around so I could be on the same side of the road as him.

It dawned on me that he was probably accustomed to vehicles passing him by because he didn't even notice me until I pulled alongside and rolled down my passenger window. He broke from his conversation, and we exchanged pleasantries. I gave him some money before both of us said nearly in unison, "God bless you."

I continued on my way. Although to a degree, it could have been an inconvenience, I didn't feel inconvenienced in the least, for it is in giving that we receive.

This man had a full head of shoulder-length brown hair parted in the middle. He had a weathered face; through his beard, I could see sharp features and a square jaw. I can only hope he saw the face of God and felt His love that day. I surely saw the face of Jesus.

Christ has no body now but yours. No hands, no feet on earth but yours. Yours are the eyes through which He looks compassion on this world. Yours are the feet with which He walks to do good. Yours are the hands with which He blesses all the world.[3]

—St. Teresa of Avila

Living with the intention of playing our part in the Body of Christ begins and continues with prayerfully considering our role, then doing our best to imitate, cooperate with, and obey Jesus. The gospels are the playbook. Please read them often. Jesus is our model. He and St. Paul have left us with instructions for living a Christ-like life:

> I have given you a model to follow, so that as I have done for you, you should also do.
> —John 13:15

> Finally, brothers, whatever is true, whatever is honorable, whatever is just, whatever is pure, whatever is lovely, whatever is gracious, if there is any excellence and if there is anything worthy of praise, think about these things. Keep on doing what you have learned and received and heard and seen in me. Then the God of peace will be with you.
> —Philippians 4:8–9

> Put on then, as God's chosen ones, holy and beloved, heartfelt compassion, kindness, humility, gentleness, and patience, bearing with one another and forgiving one another, if one has a grievance against another; as the Lord has forgiven you, so must you also do. And over

all these put on love, that is, the bond of perfection. And let the peace of Christ control your hearts, the peace into which you were also called in one body. And be thankful. Let the word of Christ dwell in you richly, as in all wisdom you teach and admonish one another, singing psalms, hymns, and spiritual songs with gratitude in your hearts to God. And whatever you do, in word or in deed, do everything in the name of the Lord Jesus, giving thanks to God the Father through him.
—Colossians 3:12–17

I know. Some of this seems impossible in the world we live in today. It's all relative, though. Jesus faced the same temptations, persecutions, ridicule, hatred, violence, and emotions we who follow Him and His teachings face today. Short of sin, Jesus has experienced everything we will ever experience; I can only imagine this is the reason He is such a patient God.

The world needs disciples of Jesus now more than ever: "whatever is true, whatever is honorable, whatever is just, whatever is pure, whatever is lovely, whatever is gracious…" must replace what is disgraceful, impure, immoral, immodest, unkind, impolite, and hostile in our communities today. And "heartfelt compassion, kindness, humility, gentleness, and patience, bearing with one another and forgiving one another…and over all these… love" must overcome the cold-heartedness, lack of compassion, civil unrest, egoism, inconsiderate behavior, violence, quick-tempers, callousness, and the unforgiving spirit we see in our streets today. Jesus needs us, the Body of Christ, to live with and exemplify these Christ-centered morals and values with the greatest intention and awareness. Right now.

Jesus is our model; as we imitate Him, we become a model for others. Paul told the Thessalonians (2 Thess. 3:9) "Rather, we wanted to present ourselves as a model for you, so that you might imitate us."

Once we commit to living with the intention of playing our part in the Body of Christ and practice the awareness that goes along with this, it will become second nature. The standard rule of thumb on the length of time it takes for something we do regularly and actively to become a habit is sixty to ninety days.

Prayerfully consider this. Before going to sleep at night, recall your actions to love your neighbor during that day and give thanks for the opportunities and awareness. Upon waking up in the morning, pray for the boldness to step forward in trust as you listen for and respond to the Holy Spirit as He shows you how to be the hands and feet of Jesus. This is our job now.

As you prepare to roll out of bed, recall the words Jesus spoke to the apostles in one of the Last Supper Discourses. "Get up, let us go" (John 14:31). Then go on, living with the intention of playing your part in the Body of Christ.

> The future starts today, not tomorrow.[4]
> —Pope St. John Paul II

By living with the intention of playing our part in the Body of Christ and being more aware of all the opportunities the Holy Spirit presents, God will fill us with the grace to embrace the call from Jesus to—Be Holy.

17
BE HOLY!

> To the church of God that is in Corinth, to you who have been sanctified in Christ Jesus, called to be holy, with all those everywhere who call upon the name of our Lord Jesus Christ, their Lord and ours.
> —1 Corinthians 1:2

> He who carries God in his heart bears heaven with him wherever he goes.
> —St. Ignatius of Loyola

> In the Body of Christ, the Holy Spirit is our Sanctifier. Stay close to Him.

Thy kingdom come, thy will be done on earth as it is in heaven. Did you know every time you pray these words, you ask Our Father to help you become holy and to live a saintly life? In the words of St. Augustine, "It would not be inconsistent with the truth to understand 'Thy will be done on earth as it is in heaven,' to mean: 'in the Church as in our Lord Jesus Christ himself.'"[1] We petition

God to make ourselves holy and ask Him to do this for the entire Church (the People of God) across the world.

Throughout the Bible, God calls us to be holy. In the Old Testament, God said to Moses:

> Speak to the whole Israelite community and tell them: Be holy, for I, the LORD your God, am holy.
> —Leviticus 19:2

God spoke similar words elsewhere in Leviticus (11:44–45; 20:7–8, 24–26), in Numbers 15:40–41, three times in Deuteronomy (14:2, 21; 26:19), and in Exodus 19:6.

In the New Testament, we are called to be holy numerous times. Jesus tells us:

> So be perfect, just as your heavenly Father is perfect.
> —Matthew 5:48

> Not everyone who says to me, "Lord, Lord," will enter the kingdom of heaven, but only the one who does the will of my Father in heaven.
> —Matthew 7:21

> If you love me, you will keep my commandments.
> —John 14:15

Please don't fret over Jesus's word "perfect" (Greek: *teleios* also means complete, mature, fully grown). According to Catholic Answers' Steven Covington, Jesus uses this word in the last verse of Matthew 5 "to demand a certain type of moral behavior that will reflect our attempt to know God fully and to therefore always seek his will in our lives."[2] It seems to be a summary and appeal centered around all His teachings in the Sermon on the Mount (Matt. Ch 5-7).

God is love; to love like Him, we need His grace. To be perfect as He is, we need to emulate His love and charity. We need to be obedient to His will and the commandments Jesus gave us to love God with all our heart, soul, mind, and strength, to love our neighbor as ourselves, and to love one another as He loves us. As St. Paul said in Romans 13:10, "Love does no evil to the neighbor; hence, love is the fulfillment of the law."

The apostles also encourage us to be holy.[3]

To be holy is to be set apart, other, and different.[4] It is to be out of this world, if you will, "to keep oneself unstained by the world" (James 1:27). St. John the Apostle wrote:

> Do not love the world or the things of the world. If anyone loves the world, the love of the Father is not in him. For all that is in the world, sensual lust, enticement for the eyes, and a pretentious life, is not from the Father but is from the world. Yet the world and its enticement are passing away. But whoever does the will of God remains forever.
>
> —1 John 2:15-17

The notes to this verse (NABRE) tell us the world as used here is "all that is hostile toward God and alienated from him. Love of the world and love of God are thus mutually exclusive." Of course, there is a multitude of things in the world that glorify God. Creation and all in it have God's handprints on them, for example. Used for good, it glorifies God. Used for evil, then it is hostile toward God.

Holiness and sanctity are interchangeable. Sanctify (or variations of the word) appears nine times in the New Testament. The Holy Spirit is our sanctifier. In everything, stay close to Him. Pope St. John Paul II tells us the way to become holy is "that of fidelity to God's will, as it is expressed to us in his Word, the commandments and the inspirations of the Holy Spirit."[5]

> What is holiness? Holiness is all the incredible things God will do in you and through you if you make yourself available to him.[6]
> —Matthew Kelly, *Amazing Possibilities*

> Holiness consists simply in doing God's will and being just what God wants us to be.
> —St. Thérèse of Lisieux

> We must make ourselves attractive to God, like our Lady. Holiness is a normal thing. Nothing extraordinary.[7]
> —St. Teresa of Calcutta

I chuckle at Mother Teresa's quote above. She makes it sound so easy! We become holy by the grace of God, albeit with the cooperation of our love and self-giving. Just as Jesus prayed after the Last Supper in his agony in the Garden of Gethsemane, we too must be willing to say, "not my will but yours be done" (Luke 22:42).

Were it not for God, it wouldn't be possible for us to be holy on our own, so relax! By His grace, we received the call to holiness at our baptism, and God has gifted us with the opportunity to become holy because He is present in the Church, the Body of Christ, and in each of us. Through His mercy, He is the fount of all holiness. By allowing His life to flow through us, we can become holy. How? Imitating Jesus and listening to Him as He speaks to us through the Holy Spirit. He will create the opportunities and equip us for holiness; we need to listen and respond.

We are all saints in the making. Age is irrelevant. The process of living a holy life is gradual. The Holy Spirit is sanctifying us from baptism to our last breath. It's a new opportunity daily and always a work in progress. We will have setbacks (selfishness, sin). By guiding us to acknowledge them, repent, and seek forgiveness, the Holy Spirit will lead us back to God's good graces, provided we cooperate.

Holiness *is* attainable, and it won't be a burden to our happiness. The state of holiness will enhance our happiness and fill us with joy. Many people think of holiness and cringe, perceiving there's no way they could accomplish this. And, if they do, they only imagine life would no longer be fun and exciting. Think about this.

"Christians do not have to turn their backs on the world in order to live in keeping with the Gospel. They should seek to find God in their own environment and try to change that environment by practicing the Christian virtues, embodying Christ's life in their own, particularly by forgiving one another" (The Navarre Bible, notes on Eph. 4:25–32).

Let's briefly look at how increasing in holiness can enhance our happiness, joy, and zeal for life.

The Fruit of the Holy Spirit

Suppose we bear the fruit of the Holy Spirit of love, joy, peace, patience, kindness, generosity, faithfulness, gentleness, and self-control in everything we do and our interactions. Why would any of this decrease our happiness?

Yes, some may look at faithfulness and realize they will need to go to church more often or pray more regularly. This will only enhance their relationship with Christ and fill them with His love, joy, and peace. Others may consider self-control and see the need to address their overeating or excessive drinking. Well, if they do and are successful, they will only be happier even though they may not be able to envision that now. How could we be less happy when any of the fruits pour out of us? This is all so attainable.

The Virtues

> For this very reason, make every effort to supplement your faith with virtue, virtue with knowledge, knowledge with self-control, self-control with endurance, endurance with devotion, devotion with mutual affection, mutual affection with love.
> —2 Peter 1:5–7

God gifted us the virtues of faith, hope, and love. Increase in these, and we will increase in holiness. To live a virtuous (morally good) life, act as Jesus did with prudence, justice, courage, and moderation. Honesty, honor, goodness, trustworthiness, humility, and respect are all virtues. The Fruit of the Holy Spirit are all virtues.

To truly love as God loves, virtuous living should be at our core. Godly love understands, admits mistakes, seeks forgiveness, shows patience, attempts to work out differences, makes amends, listens, tames the ego, and is humble. Love doesn't gossip, criticize, injure, hurt, judge, accuse, hold grudges, or berate people on social media. Loving as God loves leads to holiness. The other things are sins that cause us to fall out of holiness.

When we seek to grow in virtue, we grow in holiness, and we grow in happiness. This is all within reach.

The Beatitudes

Beatitude means happy or blessed; each is synonymous with holy. Jesus taught the Beatitudes in His Sermon on the Mount (Matt. 5:1-12). Blessed (happy, holy) are the poor in spirit, Blessed are they who mourn, and so on. In his pastoral message titled *Rejoice and be Glad – On The Call To Holiness In Today's World*,[8] I like how Pope Francis explained the Beatitudes.

"Being poor in heart: that is holiness."
"Reacting with meekness and humility: that is holiness."
"Knowing how to mourn with others: that is holiness."
"Hungering and thirsting for righteousness (justice): that is holiness."
"Seeing and acting with mercy: that is holiness."
"Keeping a heart free of all that tarnishes love: that is holiness."
"Sowing peace all around us: that is holiness."
"Accepting daily the path of the Gospel, even though it may cause us problems: that is holiness."

Indeed, those who can do these things are blessed. This is all so achievable.

When we do our best to imitate Jesus, we will grow in holiness. Devoted reading of the gospels and meditation on the life of Jesus, regular reception of Holy Communion, and frequent attendance in church are just a few blessings available that will put us on the path toward imitating Him well.

Make it a habit of reading and reflecting on the two passages highlighted in Chapter 16 on St. Paul's instruction for living a Christ-like life in Phil. 4:8–9 and Col. 3:12–17.

For some, it may be desirable to learn about the lives of some of the recognized saints. It's probably also a good idea to avoid trying to imitate them. While they all embody holiness in their unique way—abandoning themselves to the will of God and detaching from things of the world—God called them to this level of sanctification. He could ask this of you, too, although your path to holiness will be unlike any other. Here's how St. Francis de Sales viewed it:

> All of us can attain to Christian virtue and holiness, no matter in what condition of life we live and no matter what our life work may be.[9]

The word saint comes from the Latin *sanctus*, meaning "holy." God's call to holiness for you may be for living an unassuming and ordinary life with great love and humility. Or maybe this describes your classmate, colleague, or neighbor—the saint next door. I believe this describes many of the members of the Body of Christ.

The ultimate judge of someone's sainthood is God who bestows that eternal blessing the instant He welcomes a person to step into heaven with the greeting, "Well done, my good and faithful servant" (Matt. 25:21, 23).

To be saints is not a privilege for a few, but a vocation for everyone.[10]

—Pope Francis

Let us become saints so that, together on earth we will be together forever in Heaven.[11]

—St. Pio of Pietrelcina

You Are The Light of the World

Jesus spoke to them again, saying, "I am the light of the world. Whoever follows me will not walk in darkness, but will have the light of life."

—John 8:12

Speaking to His disciples, Jesus calls himself "the light of the world," then says whoever follows Him will have "the light of life." Whoever follows Him during His life on earth and into the future will have the light. Christians down through the centuries will have the light. The Body of Christ has the light.

In the Sermon on the Mount, Jesus teaches the disciples and the crowds, "You are the light of the world," that must not be hidden or covered. No, "your light must shine before others, that they may see your good deeds and glorify your heavenly Father" (Matt. 5:14–16).

Because Jesus, the light of the world and the transfigured one, lives in us, the light of His presence shines through us when we do our best to stay on the path God has planned for us. We can't help it and may not even know we are reflecting His light, radiating His love, and exuding His Spirit.

Others can tell, though. People notice. Our skin shines, our eyes clear and widen, and we smile more often and broadly. We speak gracious words. We are vibrant, energetic, and full of joy, yet peaceful and calm. There is a certain magnetism that is attractive. This attraction is Jesus Christ in the Holy Spirit flowing out of us.

Think of Moses's 40-day and night encounter with God on Mount Sinai.

> As Moses came down from Mount Sinai with the two tablets of the covenant in his hands, he did not know that the skin of his face had become radiant while he spoke with the LORD.
> —Exodus 34:29

> Be aglow in the Spirit, serve the Lord.
> —Romans 12:11 (RSV-CE)

It's now time to let your light shine! Much of what you've read in this book, when applied wherever you are in your life in your unique and creative way, will slowly turn up the dial of radiance in proportion with the grace you receive from God. You are on the radiant path of love and holiness when you actively play your part in the Body of Christ.

In his short eBook *How To Discern God's Will For Your Life* (2016, 12), Bishop Barron wrote, "Go back to the story of the burning bush in Exodus 3. We are like the bush in that the closer God gets, the more beautiful and luminous we become. We are not consumed or devoured by God's presence; we become radiant by it."

The world has become a dark place. Now more than ever, Jesus needs the Body of Christ to rise up, make disciples of all nations, and spread the message that His redeeming love, mercy, and salvation are available for everyone—all sinners, even the most hardened. God wants all humanity to be saved. He wants no one to be left out.

With Christ in us, we are the light in the darkness. Allow His love and light to shine through us. "Let us then cast off the works of darkness and put on the armor of light" (Rom. 13:12 RSV-CE). With 2.3 billion Christians in the world, all with the indwelling of the Holy Spirit, we have the power to stand up for love and shine the light on evil wherever encountered.

> A single sunbeam is enough to drive away many shadows.[12]
> —St. Francis of Assisi

Remain attached to the Vine, not letting anything threaten to weaken that hold. Be the strong branch and bear good fruit in the kingdom of God. Live continuously in the presence of Jesus in the Holy Spirit. Listen for Him with the ear of your heart and see with the eyes of faith. Receive His graces generously and share His love with others. Let your light shine for all to see.

> Live as children of light, for light produces every kind of goodness and righteousness and truth.
> —Ephesians 5:8–9

Remember, we shine so others will glorify our heavenly Father (Matt. 5:16). Always remember our Why—Jesus Christ, the Messiah, our Lord and Savior, the Resurrection and the Life, and the head of the Body of Christ. At all times, say, "Here I am Lord, I come to do your will." (Psalm 40:8a–9a). And may these words of Jesus stay on your heart and be a source of inspiration and motivation: "Behold, I am sending you" (Matt.10:16).

> Yesterday is gone. Tomorrow has not yet come. We only have today. Let us begin.[13]
> —St. Teresa of Calcutta

May the peace of Christ be with you. In Jesus' name,

Amen.

Live with the intention of playing your part in the Body of Christ so you will Shine Like the Saints we are all called to be.

NOTES

INTRODUCTION—A BIRD'S EYE VIEW

1. Elise Harris, "In Azerbaijan, Pope says faith, service weave Christian life together." *Catholic News Agency*, October 2, 2016. Pope Francis, Homily at The Church of the Immaculate Conception, Bazu, Azerbaijan, Oct. 2, 2016.

2. Fulton J. Sheen, 2015. *The Mystical Body of Christ: A Timeless Portrait Of The Church From A Beloved Catholic Evangelist,* (1935; reis., Notre Dame, Indiana: The Society for the Propagation of the Faith, Christian Classics ™, Ave Maria Press, Inc.), 37.

CHAPTER 1—CONCEPTION

1. *Compendium: Catechism of the Catholic Church* [CCCC], 2006. Washington, D.C.: United States Conference of Catholic Bishops, para. 147, p. 44.

2. Congregation for the Doctrine of Faith, *Responses to some questions regarding certain aspects of the Doctrine on the Church*, (Rome: Offices of the

Congregation for the Doctrine of the Faith, June 29, 2007), #5, confirmed by Pope Benedict XVI.

3. Joseph Cardinal Ratzinger, *Dominus Iesus*, Congregation for the Doctrine of Faith, (Rome: Offices of the Congregation for the Doctrine of the Faith, June 16, 2000), #17, confirmed by Pope John Paul II.

4. *Catechism of the Catholic Church* [CCC], 2nd ed. (Vatican City: Libreria Editrice Vaticana, 1997). para. 1256, 1272, 1284; and the *RCIA Leader's Manual*, (Alpharetta, GA: The Association for Catechumenal Ministry, 2007), pp. 187-188; Search online for 'valid baptisms' for a list of denominations considered to have valid or invalid baptisms.

5. *America's Changing Religious Landscape*; Pew Research Center, 2015. https://www.pewforum.org . Mainline Protestant denominations in America include Methodist (UMC), Lutheran (ELCA), Presbyterian, Episcopal, American Baptist, United Church of Christ, Disciples of Christ, Reformed Church, and African Methodist Episcopal (and some smaller Protestant communities).

6. Barbara A. Morgan and William J. Keimig, eds. *The RCIA Leader's Manual*. "Determining the Fact and Validity of Baptism." (The Association for Catechumenal Ministry, 2007.) Accessed 11/21/2022. https://acmrcia.org/blog/determining-fact-and-validity-baptism

7. Sheen, *The Mystical Body of Christ*, 28.

8. Ibid., 74.

9. Sheen, *The Mystical Body of Christ*, 76.

Chapter 2—Circulation

1. *The Word Among Us*, 2019. "Mass Reading and Meditation," (Frederick, MD: The Word Among Us). Meditation for July 27, 2019, taken from The Word Among Us magazine (wau.org). Used with permission. https://wau.org/meditations/2019/07/27/.

2. National Library of Medicine; 2010. https://www.ncbi.nlm.nih.gov/books/NBK279250/ Last updated January 31, 2019. Accessed July 8, 2022.

3. *Britannica,* s.v. "Capillary (anatomy)," accessed July 8, 2022, https://www.britannica.com/science/capillary.

4. University of Minnesota, n.d., *Atlas of Human Cardiac Anatomy:* Physiology Tutorial > blood vessels, accessed July 8, 2022, http://www.vhlab.umn.edu/atlas/physiology-tutorial/blood-vessels.shtml.

5. Ibid.

6. Lynne Eldridge, MD, n.d., "Capillary Structure and Function in the Body," Very Well Health Last updated December 14, 2021. https://verywellhealth.com/.

7. Britannica, s.v. "Capillary."

8. Jill Seladi-Schulman, Ph.D, 2019. "Capillaries and their Functions." Healthline, March 12, 2019. https://www.healthline.com/health/function-of-capillaries#functions.

9. "Capillary Beds: Definition & Functions." Study.com. November 4, 2015. https://study.com/academy/lesson/capillary-beds-definition-functions.html.

10. University of Rochester Medical Center, n.d. *Health Encyclopedia,* "What is Plasma?" https://www.urmc.

rochester.edu/encyclopedia/content.aspx?ContentType ID=160&ContentID=37. Accessed July 8, 2022.

11. Seladi-Schulman, Ph.D, 2019. "Capillaries and their Functions."

12. Susan Eymann, MS, 2015. "11 Fascinating Blood Flow Facts from the Human Body" Transonic: Sensing Savvy (blog). December 9, 2015. Source: The Incredible Machine (1992), National Geographic Society, Washington, D.C., https://blog.transonic.com/human-interest/blood-flow-facts-human-body.

13. Bailey, Regina. 2019. "Red Blood Cells (Erythrocytes): Structure, Function, and Related Disorders." ThoughtCo. Last updated July 28, 2019. https://www.thoughtco.com/red-blood-cells-373487.

14. Bailey, 2019. "8 Types of White Blood Cells." ThoughtCo. Last updated November 27, 2019. https://www.thoughtco.com/types-of-white-blood-cells-373374.

15. University of Rochester Medical Center, n.d. *Health Encyclopedia*, "What are White Blood Cells?" Medical Reviewers: L Renee Watson, MSN RN, Raymond Turley Jr. PA-C, Todd Gersten, MD. Accessed July 10, 2022. https://www.urmc.rochester.edu/encyclopedia/content.aspx?ContentTypeID=35&ContentID=160.

16. Perrin Braun, 2022. "High White Blood Cell Count? What You Should Know." Inside Tracker: The Inside Track (blog). Last updated July 9, 2020. https://blog.insidetracker.com/45247913486-high-white-blood-cell-count-what-you-should/.

17. Julianne Chiaet, 2016. "White Blood Cell Types and Functions." Labroots. April 16, 2016, accessed July 10,

2022. https://www.labroots.com/trending/videos/9734/white-blood-cell-types-functions/.

18. Williams, Dr. Marlene. "What Are Platelets And Why Are They Important?" Johns Hopkins Medicine, accessed July 10, 2022. https://www.hopkinsmedicine.org/heart_vascular_institute/centers_excellence/women_cardiovascular_health_center/patient_information/health_topics/platelets.html

CHAPTER 3—CONNECTION

1. St Augustine, Sermo 267, 4: PL 38, 1231D, quoted in *Catechism of the Catholic Church*, 797.

2. Thomas Aquinas, *Summa Theologiae*, trans. Fathers of the English Dominican Province (New York: Benzinger Brothers, 191-1925), III, q. 8, a. 1, ad. 3.

3. Pope Francis, *Evangelii Gaudium—The Joy of the Gospel*, (Washington D.C., United States Conference of Catholic Bishops, 2013). Apostolic Exhortation, 40. Vatican website, November 24, 2013. https://www.vatican.va/content/francesco/en/apost_exhortations/documents/papa-francesco_esortazione-ap_20131124_evangelii-gaudium.html.

4. *The Word Among Us*, 2018. "Mass Reading and Meditation," (Frederick, MD: The Word Among Us). Meditation for July 13, 2018, taken from The Word Among Us magazine (wau.org). Used with permission https://wau.org/meditations/2018/07/13/.

5. CCC 738, 195. St Cyril of Alexandria, *In Jo. ev.*, 11, 11: PG74, 561.

6. Jeff Diamant, 2019. "News in the Numbers," Facttank. (Washington, DC: Pew Research Center). https://www.pewresearch.org.

7. Pope Francis: Daily Inspirations for 2018 Daily Calendar. (Portland, ME: Sellers Publishing, Inc.), From: Address to a national conference of prison chaplains, the Vatican, October 23, 2012.

CHAPTER 4—UNIQUE

1. Worldometers.info/world-population.

2. Anahad O'Connor, The New York Times: "The Claim: Identical Twins Have Identical Fingerprints." *The New York Times*, November 2, 2004.

3. Pope Francis, *365 Daily Meditations With Pope Francis.* "The Gift of Parenthood." (Washington, DC: United States Conference of Catholic Bishops, 2014) 344, December 9 Devotional: Address to the National Numerous Family Association, Paul VI Audience Hall. December 28, 2014. (Vatican City: Libreria Editrice Vaticana).

4. University of Navarre, The Navarre Bible (Princeton: Scepter Publishers, 2001), New Testament: Compact Edition, (RSV-CE), commentary by members of the Faculty of Theology of the University of Navarre, notes on 1 Corinthians 12:1-11, p. 436.

5. Pope Francis (@Ponitfex), "During this missionary month, the Lord is also calling you: He is asking you to be a gift wherever you are, just as you are, with everyone around you. Courage! The Lord expects great things from you!" Twitter, October 21, 2019, 9:31a.m. https://twitter.com/pontifex/status/1186243230821568512.

6. St. Josemaria Escrivá, *Hom.*, 2, 47, quoted in The Navarre Bible 2001, notes on Matthew 25:14–30 pp. 70-71.

7. Kendra Cherry, "The Amount of Personality Traits That Exist." verywellmind. Last updated on December 14, 2020. http://www.verywellmind.com/how-many-personality-traits-are-there- 2795430

8. Mother M. Angelica, 1977. *Jesus Needs Me*, (Hanceville, AL: Our Lady of the Angels Monastery).

9. Matthew Kelly, *Amazing Possibilities: 365 Daily Devotions*, 1st ed. (Palm Beach, FL: Blue Sparrow Books, 2020). Devotional for December 22, 379.

10. Sheen, *The Mystical Body of Christ*, 218.

CHAPTER 5—DESTINY

1. Bishop Robert Barron, "Friends, today's Gospel focuses on the faith of the four men who brought a paralytic to Jesus for healing." Facebook, January 12, 2018. https://www.facebook.com/profile/100044229589504/search/?q=Friends%2C%20today%27s%20Gospel%20focuses%20on%20the%20faith%20of%20four%20men.

2. Pope Francis (@Pontifex), "Every time we give in to selfishness and say "No" to God, we spoil his loving plan for us." Twitter, May 26, 2013, 6:26 a.m. https://twitter.com/pontifex/status/338601910737186817.

3. Bishop Robert Barron and Brandon Vogt, "How To Discern God's Will For Your Life," April 19, 2016, in The Word on Fire Show, produced by Word on Fire, podcast, episode WOF 019, MP3 audio, 27:02,

https://www.wordonfire.org/videos/wordonfire-show/episode19/.

4. Bishop Robert Barron, "What is Love?" Sunday Sermons, January 28, 2007, Homily – Cycle C – Ordinary Time – Week 4. Published by: wordonfire.org. MP3 audio, 4:35, https://www.wordonfire.org/videos/sermons/what-is-love/.

5. Barron, "What is Love?" 4:42.

6. Pope Francis, *Encountering Truth: Meeting God in the Everyday. The Morning Homilies from St. Martha's Chapel*, (New York: Image, 2015), 290.

7. *The Word Among Us*, "Mass Reading and Meditation," (Frederick, MD: The Word Among Us, 2017). Meditation for July 25, 2017, The Word Among Us magazine (wau.org). Used with permission https://www.wau.org/meditations/2017/07/25/.

8. Bishop Robert Barron, "Lenten Gospel Reflections." Wordonfire.org. (Des Plaines, IL: Word on Fire, May 20, 2022). On Luke 13:1-9. https://www.wordonfire.org/reflections/lent/c-lent-wk3-sunday/?queryID=7d5eba9c987acace24679097e84c1322.

9. Bishop Robert Barron, *Daily Gospel Reflections*, "Friends, in our Gospel Jesus tells us that if we had faith the size of a mustard seed." Facebook, July 31, 2017. https://www.facebook.com/permalink.php?story_fbid=1480414508664338&id=179690545403414&comment_id=1490105687695220.

10. Dom Hubert Van Zeller, "Give Yourself Joyfully to God". Catholic Exchange, September 9, 2016. Article from a chapter in Dom Van Zeller's book *How to Find*

God . . . And Discover Your True Self in the Process, (Nashua, NH: Sophia Institute Press, 1998).

11. Actual quote from St. Catherine: "If you are what you ought to be, you will set fire to all Italy, and not only yonder." Source: Benincasa, Catherine. *Saint Catherine of Siena As Seen In Her Letters*, trans. Vida Scudder (New York: E.P. Dutton, 1906), 305. Internet Archive. https://archive.org/details/saintcatherineof0000cath/page/n9/mode/2up.

12. Kelly, *Amazing Possibilities*, 385. Devotional for December 28.

CHAPTER 6—POTENTIAL

1. Fr. Michael Van Sloun, "The Power of the Holy Spirit at Confirmation." The Catholic Spirit, May 23, 2018. https://thecatholicspirit.com/faith/focus-on-faith/faith-fundamentals/the-power-of-the-holy-spirit-at-confirmation/.

2. Van Sloun, "Gifts and fruits of the Holy Spirit" The Catholic Spirit, February 17, 2011. http://www.thecatholicspirit.com.

3. Bishop Robert Barron (@bishopbarron), "Your life is not about you. It's about what the Holy Spirit wants to accomplish through you." Instagram, May 29, 2020, Mass from Bishop Barron's Chapel. https://www.instagram.com/stories/highlights/17869750147651116/.

4. *The Word Among Us*, "Mass Reading and Meditation." (Frederick, MD: The Word Among Us, 2021). Meditation for January 7, 2021, taken from The Word Among Us magazine (wau.org). Used with permission. https://www.wau.org/meditations/2021/01/07/180532/.

Chapter 7—Unified

1. Heart Matters Magazine, n.d. "Watch: How are blood vessels made?" London: British Heart Foundation. https://www.bhf.org.uk.

2. The Lutheran World Federation and the Roman Catholic Church, "Joint Declaration on the Doctrine of Justification." (Geneva: The Lutheran World Federation, 2019).

3. Dr Adam DeVille, "Two Paton Saints of Christian Unity", The Catholic World Report, 2014. https://www.catholicworldreport.com/2014/04/28/two_patron_saints_of_christian_unity/.

4. *The Word Among Us*, "Mass Reading and Meditation," (Frederick, MD: The Word Among Us). Meditation for October 28, 2019, taken from The Word Among Us magazine (wau.org). Used with permission. https://www.wau.org/meditations/2019/10/28/.

5. Pope Francis, *365 Daily Meditations with Pope Francis*, "Christian Unity." (Washington D.C., United States Conference of Catholic Bishops, 2015), 87. March 27 devotional. Quote from Homily at Celebration of Vespers on the Conversion of St. Paul the Apostle. Basilica of St Paul Outside the Walls. January 25, 2015 (Vatican City State: Libreria Editrice Vaticana).

6. Sheen, *The Mystical Body of Christ*, 242.

7. Sheen, *The Mystical Body of Christ*, 74.

8. Cna. "Pope Says Everyone Can Do Good, Regardless of Belief." (Vatican City, Catholic News Agency, May 22, 2013). https://www.catholicnewsagency.com/news/27286/pope-says-everyone-can-do-good-regardless-of-belief.

NOTES

9. Catholic News Agency, "Everyone Can Do Good."

10. Pius XII, encyclical, *Mystici Corporis*: DS 3808. Neuner, Jsef, SJ, and Dupuis, Jacques, SJ, eds, *The Christian Faith: Doctrinal Documents of the Catholic Church*, 5th ed., (New York: Alba House, 1992), quoted in *Catechism of the Catholic Church*, 797.

11. Sheen, *The Mystical Body of Christ*, 290.

12. Mother M. Angelica, *Jesus Needs Me*. (Hanceville, AL: Our Lady of the Angels Monastery, 1977).

13. Barron, *Daily Gospel Reflections* on Luke 9:1–6. September 23, 2020. Des Plaines, IL: Word on Fire Catholic Ministries, 2020. Received in Gmail.

14. St. Cyril of Alexandria, IN Jo. ev., 11, 11: PG 74, 561, quoted in *Catechism of the Catholic Church* 738.

Chapter 8—Nutrients

1. VisibleBody.com, 2020; *"Functions of the Blood: 8 Facts about Blood"*; https://www.visiblebody.com/learn/circulatory/circulatory-functions-of-the-blood

2. Sheen, *The Mystical Body of Christ*, 38.

3. Consulted and paraphrased these sources for the Seven Gifts of the Holy Spirit:

    Thomas Aquinas: The Gifts of the Spirit: Selected Spiritual Writings. Selected by Benedict Ashley, O.P. New City Press, 1995.

    Thomas Aquinas, 1485. *Summa Theologiae*. Benziger Brothers Printers to the Holy Apostolic See, Publisher. Published in English 1911.

Diocese of Lafayette, n.d., "Gifts and Charisms: Gifts and Charisms of the Holy Spirit". Diocese of Lafayette, LA. https://diolaf.org/gifts-and-charisms.

Fr. Frank Blisard, 2019. "The Seven Gifts of the Holy Spirit: What are the seven gifts of the Holy Spirit, and why do they matter?" San Diego: Catholic Answers. https://www.catholic.com/magazine/print-edition/the-seven-gifts-of-the-holy-spirit/.

Cameron, Fr. Peter John, O.P., *The Gifts of the Holy Spirit According to Saint Thomas Aquinas*. (New Haven, CT: Catholic Information Service, Knights of Columbus Supreme Council, 2002).

4. Fr. John Gabage, Pastor, *St. Christopher Parish Bulletin*, (Chester, MD: St. Christopher's Church, October 6, 2019).

5. Rick Warren, *The Purpose Driven Life: What on Earth Am I Here For?* (Grand Rapids: Zondervan, 2002).

6. Consulted and paraphrased these sources for the Nine Fruits of the Holy Spirit:

St Thomas Aquinas, 1485. *Summa Theologiae*. Benziger Brothers Printers to the Holy Apostolic See, Publisher. Published in English 1911. (I/II 70.3).

Fr. Michael Van Sloan, 2020. "The Fruits of the Holy Spirit." The Catholic Spirit. St. Paul, MN, Archdiocese of St Paul & MLPS, October 15, 2020. https://thecatholicspirit.com/faith/focus-on-faith/faith-fundamentals/the-fruits-of-the-holy-spirit/.

Scripture Catholic, n.d. "The Fruits and Gifts From the Holy Spirit and Their Meanings" https://www.scripturecatholic.com/the-fruits-and-gifts-from-the-holy-spirit/.

NOTES

7. Barron, *Daily Gospel Reflections* on Luke 13:1–9. (Des Plaines, IL: Word on Fire Catholic Ministries, October 24, 2020). Received in Gmail.

8. Barron, *Daily Gospel Reflections* on Mark 7:1–13. February 9, 2021, Word on Fire.

9. Pope Francis, *365 Daily Meditations with Pope Francis*, 239. "Joyful Christians," August 26 devotional. From @Pontifex, Twitter, February 13, 2014, 3:30 a.m.

10. Msgr. Stuart Swetland, "A Primer on Peace," (San Diego: Catholic Answers, 2007). https://www.catholic.com/magazine/print-edition/a-primer-on-peace.

11. Pope Francis, *365 Daily Meditations with Pope Francis*, 263. "Receive Peace," September 19 devotional. Message to the Vicar General for the Diocese of Rome, July 19, 2013, (Vatican City State: Libreria Editrice Vaticana).

12. Fulton J. Sheen, Catholic-Link.org (@catholiclink_en). 2018. "Never measure your generosity by what you give, but rather by what you have left." Twitter, March 23, 2018, 4:00 p.m. https://twitter.com/catholiclink_en/status/977273872985845760

13. Bill Wegner, *Dare to Be Holy*: *12 Fruits of the Holy Spirit*. (Howell, NJ: Good News International, 2005). St. Mary Mystical Rose Parish, Armada, MI.

14. Caccioppoli Family website, updated February 21, 2022. "Padre Pio: My Life For Each Of You." https://www.caccioppoli.com/index.htm, accessed July 25, 2022, and "Padre Pio's Words," https://caccioppoli.com/Padre%20Pio%20words.html, accessed July 25, 2022.

15. Sheen, *The Mystical Body of Christ*, 206.

Chapter 9—Nourishment

1. Matthew 14:13–21, 15:32–39; Mark 6:33–44, 8:1–10; Luke 9:10–17; John 6:1–15.

2. Second Vatican Council, "Dogmatic Constitution on the Church, *Lumen Gentium* [*LG 5*], 1964," quoted in *Catechism of the Catholic Church*, 567.

3. *Compendium—Catechism of the Catholic Church*, 107.

4. *Compendium—Catechism of the Catholic Church*, 590.

5. Pope Francis, Daily Calendar – August 11/12, 2018. (New York: Sellers Publishing, Inc., 2018). From @Pontifex, Twitter, November 13, 2016, 7:03a.m.

6. USCCB Committee on Evangelization, 2002. "Go and Make Disciples: A National Plan and Strategy for Catholic Evangelization in the United States." What is Evangelization? para. 17.

7. Barron, *Daily Gospel Reflections* on Luke 10:1–9. (Des Plaines, IL: Word on Fire Catholic Ministries, October18, 2019). Received in Gmail.

8. Dr. Tim Gray, "Spiritual Wealth" – Formed: Daily Reflections video from February 24, 2022. (Greenwood Village, CO: Augustine Institute, 2022).

Chapter 10—Healthy Heart

1. Barron, 2019. *Daily Gospel Reflections* on Luke 10:1–9, October18, 2019.

NOTES

Chapter 11—Good Fruits

1. Matthew Kelly, *Perfectly Yourself: Discovering God's Dream for You.* (North Palm Beach, FL: Blue Sparrow Publishing, 2017) 167.

2. Quote Investigator, n.d. "Take the first step in faith. You don't have to see the whole staircase, just take the first step." Accessed July 22, 2022. Quote attributed to Martin Luther King Jr. Reference: 1991 May-June, Mother Jones, Volume 16, Number 31, Kids First! by Marian Wright Edelman, Start Page 31, Quote Page 77, Published by the Foundation for National Progress, San Francisco, California. https://quoteinvestigator.com/2019/04/18/staircase/.

3. Pope Francis, *365 Daily Meditations with Pope Francis,* 118, "Reaching Fullness," April 27 devotional: Address at the Plenary Session of the Pontifical Academy of Sciences. Casina of Pius IV, October 27, 2014, (Vatican City State: Libreria Editrice Vaticana).

4. Catholic News Agency, "Pope Urges Christians to Remember Final Judgement." Vatican City, Catholic News Agency, April 24, 2013. https://www.catholicnewsagency.com/news/27071/pope-urges-christians-to-remember-final-judgment/.

5. Scott Hahn, *A Father Who Keeps His Promises: God's Covenant Love in Scripture.* (Columbus, OH, Servant, an imprint of Franciscan Media, 1998), 74.

6. St. Francis de Sales and Jane de Chantel, n.d. *Francis de Sales, Jane de Chantal: Letters of Spiritual Direction,* 111. Peronne Marie Thibert, VHM, trans., Wendy M. Wright and Joseph F. Power, O.S.F.S. editors. (Mahwah, NJ: Paulist Press, 1988), 111.

Chapter 12—Little Greatness

1. Consulted and Paraphrased from: The Society of the Little Flower: "Who Is St. Therese?" https://www.littleflower.org and Wikipedia https://en.wikipedia.org/wiki/Th%C3%A9r%C3%A8se_of_Lisieux.

2. John Burger, "'Do Ordinary Things With Extraordinary Love:' The Things That Made Mother Teresa Tick." *National Catholic Register*, August 26, 2010, accessed July 22, 2022, https://www.ncregister.com/news/do-ordinary-things-with-extraordinary-love.

3. *Catechism of the Catholic Church* 961. Refers to the term "communion of saints", that which Christians who pray the Apostles Creed profess a belief in and affirm. The interpretation of the term between Christian denominations differs, however.

4. Loren Renz and Leslie Marino, *Giving in the Aftermath of 9/11*, (New York: The Foundation Center, 2003). https://foundationcenter.org/gainknowledge/research/pdf/9_11update03.pdf.

Chapter 13—As Yourself

1. The bible verse "Love your neighbor as yourself" appears in Leviticus 19:18, Matthew 22:39, Matthew 19:19, Mark 12:31, Luke 10:27, James 2:8, and Romans 13:9.

2. God In All Things, 2015. "The 'As Yourself' Part of the Commandment to Love Your Neighbor." Feb. 14, 2015, God In All Things (blog), posted by guest. Accessed July 23, 2022. www.godinallthings.com.

3. Found in verses Matthew 16:24, Luke 9:23, Mark 8:34.

4. Caccioppoli, n.d. "Padre Pio's Words." https://caccioppoli.com/Padre%20Pio%20words.html
5. Mother Angelica, *Mother Angelica on Suffering and Burnout*, (Irondale, AL: EWTN Publishing, Inc., 2016), 271.
6. Pope Francis, *365 Daily Meditations with Pope Francis*, 267. "Watch Out for Gossip." September 23 devotional: Address and Presentation of Christmas Greetings to the Roman Curia. Clementine Hall. December 22, 2014, (Vatican City State: Libreria Editrice Vaticana).

CHAPTER 14—IN COMMUNION

1. John Paul II, Apostolic Journey To Poland, Holy Mass. Homily Of His Holiness John Paul II. Victory Square, Warsaw, June 2, 1979. (Vatican City: Libreria Editrice Vaticana, 1979).
2. Sheen, *The Mystical Body of Christ*, 290.
3. Kelly, Matthew, *Rediscover Catholicism: A Spiritual Guide to Living with Passion & Purpose.* (North Palm Beach, FL: Blue Sparrow, 2010).
4. Judith Bennett, n.d. "Who was Who at the Council." United Kingdom: Vatican II–Voice of The Church. Updated November 15, 2021. https://vatican2voice.org.
5. Fr. John Crossin, "The Ecumenical Movement: A School for Virtue." Appeared in the Catholic News Service: Faith Alive (blog), Fall, 2012. Vatican II and the Ecumenical Movement. https://www.usccb.org/committees/ecumenical-interreligious-affairs/vatican-ii-and-ecumenical-movement.

6. Paul VI, "Documents of Vatican II: Decree of the Apostolate of the Laity," *Apostolicam Actuositatem.* (Vatican City: the Holy See, 18 November 1965). Vatican Council II: Constitutions, Decrees, Declarations—The Basic Sixteen Documents, edited by Austin Flannery, OP, © 1996. Used with permission of Liturgical Press, Collegeville, Minnesota.

7. *Apostolicam Actuositatem*, Chapter III, sec. 11.

8. *Apostolicam Actuositatem*, Chapter III, sec. 12.

9. *Apostolicam Actuositatem*, Chapter I, sec. 2.

10. Msgr. Owen Campion, "The Church is the Mystical Body of Christ." (South Bend, IN: Today's Catholic, Diocese of Fort Wayne, 2014).

Chapter 15—Never Alone

1. Pietro Molla and Elio Guerriero, *Saint Gianna Molla: Wife, Mother, Doctor.* (San Francisco: Ignatius Press, 2004).

2. Sister M. Benedicta Clauss, O.S.B, *God Calls the Walsh Family.* (Utica, NY: McDowell Publications, 2006).

3. Notes on 1 Corinthians 2:13 (NABRE) "In spiritual terms: the Spirit teaches spiritual people a new mode of perception (1 Cor 2:12) and an appropriate language by which they can share their self-understanding, their knowledge about what God has done in them."

4. Second Vatican Council, "Pastoral Constitution of the Church in the Modern World, *Gaudium et Spes*, December 7, 1965," (Vatican City: Papal Archive, The Holy See, 1965). https://www.vatican.va/archive/hist_councils/ii_vatican_council/documents/

vat-ii_cons_19651207_gaudium-et-spes_en.html. (trans. and quoted in *Catechism of the Catholic Church*, 2nd ed., 1776, [United States Catholic Conference, Inc.: Libreria Editrice Vaticana: 1994]).

CHAPTER 16—BE ALIVE

1. Sheen, *The Mystical Body of Christ*, 217.
2. Penguin Books India, *Mother Teresa: 100 Inspirational Quotes*. (United Kingdom, Penguin Books Limited, 2016), 4.
3. Quote from the poem *Christ Has No Body* that is widely attributed to St. Teresa of Avila although it doesn't appear in any of her published writings.
4. Pope John Paul II Quotes. BrainyQuote.com, Brainy Media Inc, 2022. https://www.brainyquote.com/quotes/pope_john_paul_ii_178863, accessed July 24, 2022.

CHAPTER 17—BE HOLY

1. St. Augustine, *De serm. Dom.* 2,6,24: PL 34, 1279, quoted in *Catechism of the Catholic Church*, 2827.
2. Steven Covington, "Be Perfect" (San Diego: Catholic Answers, 1999).
3. See: 1 Cor. 1:2; 1 Pet. 1:14–16; Col. 3:12–13; Rom 6:22-23; Eph. 4:22–24; 1 Thess. 5:23, 1 Thess. 3:11–13, Jas. 1:27.
4. Barron, Robert, "Who Is God?" Sunday Sermons: May 20, 2022. (Des Plaines, IL: Word on Fire Catholic Ministries, 2022). wordonfire.org. https://www.wordonfire.org/videos/sermons/who-is-god/.

5. John Paul II, "Man Is Sanctified by the Holy Spirit", *L'Osservatore Romano.* Vatican City: Libreria Editrice Vaticana, July 29, 1998). This item 648 digitally provided courtesy CatholicCulture.org: Trinity Communications, 2022.

6. Kelly, *Amazing Possibilities*, 127. Daily devotional for April 26.

7. Franciscan Media, n.d., "Holy Quotes From Mother Teresa." Franciscan Media: Franciscan Spirit (blog). Accessed July 24, 2022. https://www.franciscanmedia.org/franciscan-spirit-blog/holy-quotes-from-mother-teresa.

8. Pope Francis, *Gaudete Et Exsultate (Rejoice and Be Glad) – On The Call To Holiness In Today's World.* (Vatican City: Dicastero per la Comunicazione - Libreria Editrice Vaticana, 2018). Chapter Three, para. 70, 74, 76, 79, 82, 86, 89, 94.

9. CatholicSaints.Info, "Saint Francis de Sales." Updated February 25, 2022, accessed July 27, 2022. https://catholicsaints.info/saint-francis-de-sales/.

10. Pope Francis (@Ponitfex). 2013. "To be saints is not a privilege for the few, but a vocation for everyone." Twitter, November 21, 2013, 9:21 a.m. https://twitter.com/pontifex/status/403528682800562176?lang=en.

11. Caccioppoli, n.d. "Padre Pio's Words." https://caccioppoli.com/Padre%20Pio%20words.html.

12. Jon M. Sweeney, *The Complete Francis of Assisi: His Life, The Complete Writings, and The Little Flowers.* (Brewster, MA: Paraclete Press, 2015).

13. Mother Teresa, *In the Heart of the World: Thoughts, Stories & Prayers,* (Novato, CA: New World Library, 2010), 17.

ABOUT THE AUTHOR

Marty Mitchell is a Catholic Christian author, speaker, and illuminator who has a passion for helping Christians understand and play their unique part in the body of Christ so they can be filled with the love, joy, happiness, and peace of God that comes from living their Best Blessed Life™.

Marty grew up in a Navy family alternating between the Pacific and Atlantic coasts. He went to high school and college in Virginia where he received a degree in Finance before a thirty-year career in the capital markets. He is a practicing Catholic Christian today although his faith journey didn't always take a straight path.

For a couple decades, his lifestyle revolved around living for the next party. During this time, he strayed from practicing his faith and wasn't living a Christ-centered life. Certain there was more to life, Marty went on a Holy Spirit led spiritual journey to understand his purpose in life by exploring the body of Christ and the role he was expected to play in it. This experience transformed him by clarifying his God-given purpose, drawing him into a deeper relationship with God, and increasing his self-worth, intention, and love for life.

Today, in his writing, speaking, and coaching, Marty illuminates the messages of Love and Christian unity, as well as the uniqueness and great potential of all of God's children by shining a light on their God-given gifts and talents and on all their goodness. He lives in Maryland near the shores of Chesapeake Bay and enjoys his faith, spending time with family and friends, golfing, boating, fishing, and creating laughter.

Connect with me at MartyMitchell.me

Your Next Best Steps Toward Playing Your Part in the Body of Christ

1. Are you living your Best Blessed Life? Take the 'Shine Like a Saint!' Assessment and grab the FREE BONUS that is waiting for you when you're finished.

2. Use the free chapter-by-chapter Questions for Reflection PDF for your personal use, in a group or church study, or in your The Capillaries of Christ Book Club.

3. Become a part of the Illuminated Souls Community: Join other Christ-centered souls in sharing and receiving support, encouragement, ideas, and opportunities for collaboration in the Body of Christ, and much more!

4. Sign up for the 'Shine Like a Saint!' Course (see next page for details). Complimentary membership in the Illuminated Souls Community is included while taking this course.

https://www.martymitchell.me

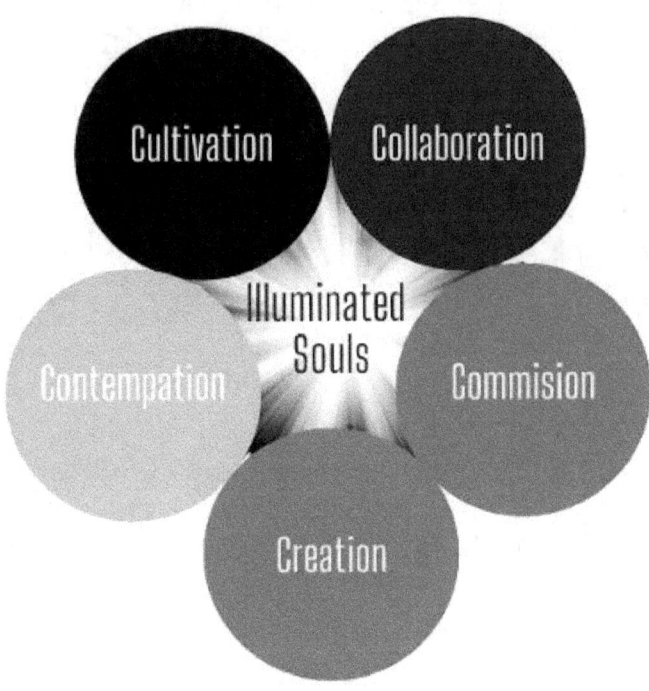

The 'Shine Like A Saint!' Course is available in these formats:

12-Week Online Self-Study with videos, study guides, and action steps
12-Week Mastermind: 10 Seat Limit, Live Coaching, 90-minute Sessions
Live Illumination Sessions: Small Group & Family Coaching
Live 5-hour Workshops—unlimited seating

For more information please visit: www.martymitchell.me/shine-like-a-saint
Or contact me at marty@martymitchell.me

Marty Mitchell
SHINE LIKE A SAINT!

www.ingramcontent.com/pod-product-compliance
Lightning Source LLC
LaVergne TN
LVHW010155070526
838199LV00062B/4367